PRACTICAL SOCIAL WORK

Series Editor: Jo Campling

BASW

Editorial Advisory Board:
Terry Bamford, Malcolm Payne, Patrick Phelan,
Peter Riches, Daphne Statham, Jane Tunstill,
Sue Walrond-Skinner and Margaret Yelloly

Social work is at an important stage in its development. All professions must be responsive to changing social and economic conditions if they are to meet the needs of those they serve. This series focuses on sound practice and the specific contribution which social workers can make to the well-being of our society.

The British Association of Social Workers has always been conscious of its role in setting guidelines for practice and in seeking to raise professional standards. The conception of the Practical Social Work series arose from a survey of BASW members to discover where they, the practitioners in social work, felt there was the most need for new literature. The response was overwhelming and enthusiastic, and the result is a carefully planned, coherent series of books. The emphasis is firmly on practice, set in a theoretical framework. The books will inform, stimulate and promote discussion, thus adding to the further development of skills and high professional standards. All the authors are practitioners and teachers of social work representing a wide variety of experience.

JO CAMPLING

PRACTICAL SOCIAL WORK

Series Editor: Jo Campling

BASW

Problems of Childhood and Adolescence

Michael Kerfoot and Alan Butler

MACMILLAN
EDUCATION

First published 1988

Published by
MACMILLAN EDUCATION LTD
Houndmills, Basingstoke, Hampshire RG21 2XS
and London
Companies and representatives
throughout the world

Printed in Hong Kong

British Library Cataloguing in Publication Data
Kerfoot, Michael
Problems of childhood and adolescence.—
(Practical social work).
1. Social work with youth—Great Britain
I. Title II. Butler, Alan III. Series
362.7'042'0941   HV1441.G7
ISBN 0-333-42070-5 (hardcover)
ISBN 0-333-42071-3 (paperback)

For Ben, Christy and Matthew

Series Standing Order

If you would like to receive future titles in this series as they are published,
you can make use of our standing order facility. To place a standing order
please contact your bookseller or, in case of difficulty, write to us at the
address below with your name and address and the name of the series.
Please state with which title you wish to begin your standing order. (If you
live outside the United Kingdom we may not have the rights for your area,
in which case we will forward your order to the publisher concerned.)

Customer Services Department, Macmillan Distribution Ltd,
Houndmills, Basingstoke, Hampshire, RG21 2XS, England.

Contents

Acknowledgements

We would like to thank colleagues who have assisted in the preparation of this book, especially Elizabeth Glynn and Brian Minty. Secretarial support has been supplied by Madelaine Richardson, Susan Walker and Kamaljeet Chagger, for which we are grateful.

Finally, for their intellectual inspiration, patience and unstinting support we are indebted to Penny Kerfoot and Barbara J. Hudson.

MICHAEL KERFOOT
ALAN BUTLER

1

Introduction

In this book we have attempted to address some of the issues in the assessment of, and intervention in, the problems of childhood and adolescence. Social workers are required to explore and assess a complex variety of situations in which distressed children find themselves, and to develop a range of responses. To accomplish these tasks effectively social workers are required to develop an understanding of normal child development; a grasp of the common problems evidenced in childhood and adolescence; and a broad appreciation of the influence that the family and wider environmental factors may have upon such problems.

Over the past decade specialist pyschiatric services for children and adolescents have developed very rapidly. From this growth has emerged a great deal of research-based information, and innovative methods of intervention. However, many of the skills necessary to respond to disturbance in children and adolescents remain locked within the specialist services. We believe that much of this knowledge and skill could easily be generalised to the wider social work profession. They are just as relevant to the generic social worker engaged in 'child care' cases within the area team, or to those working with children in various residential establishments.

Whilst drawing upon this body of knowledge we do not intend this to be a textbook of child psychiatry. Many such books already exist and we make reference to them in the Further Reading section at the end of the book. Rather, it is designed to be a practical guide for social workers who may be

1

confronted by difficult or disturbed children in their daily work. Our aim is that it will enable them to analyse situations with increased confidence and clarity, comprehend some of the underlying causal factors, assess difficulties more appropriately, and intervene more effectively. It should also give them a realistic appreciation of the limits of their own expertise, and an indication as to the point at which it may be more appropriate to refer the child to another specialist agency.

The chapters follow a broadly similar format throughout the book. We begin each chapter by defining the area that we intend to examine and then looking at the prevalance of the problem. This is followed by a section which examines some of the theoretical models of understanding that are current. In this, we have drawn widely upon research and opinion which we hope will be both interesting and stimulating to social workers. We then look at the ways in which the problem might be appropriately managed by a social worker. Finally, we conclude each chapter with some key summary points, and a short case study drawn from our own practice by way of illustration.

In the next chapter, we begin by exploring the professional context within which child and adolescent problems are identified and responded to, and look at some of the issues which have, in the past, divided specialist services from the more generic children's services. From this starting point we proceeed developmentally, chapter by chapter, to examine problems which commonly occur during childhood and adolescence, and which may well require some form of professional help.

In Chapters 3 and 4 we consider some of the most common problems of the childhood period – eating, sleeping, and toileting difficulties – and we examine these in the light of developmental norms, the emotional conflict that they provoke, and the external factors which impinge upon the family.

In Chapter 5 we examine some of the common emotional problems of childhood such as anxiety, fears, phobias, and depression. In many cases these may be transitory and self-limiting. However, if they persist then skilled assessment and intervention may become necessary.

Some aspects of a young person's behaviour may be seen as objectionable by other people. Many will fall foul of various authority figures, even the Law. In Chapter 6 we examine so-called anti-social or conduct problems and look at some of the theories that have been advanced to explain them. We examine the relevance of such theory to social work practice and look at some possible ways of managing the problems.

A large number of children miss significant parts of their school life. In Chapter 7 we review the broad and complex area of school attendance problems, and the different forms that these can take. Both family and school influences play an important part in the causation and maintenance of these difficulties and we discuss these factors and their importance for the child's future development.

In Chapter 8 we examine an increasing problem, that of anorexia nervosa. Its occurrence is often dramatic, and profoundly worrying both for the individual and for other family members. Unlike many of the problems that we refer to in this book, anorexia nervosa results, almost inevitably, in a psychiatric assessment and subsequent in-patient treatment. However, this does not mean the social worker is excluded from the management of the case. We consider the various clinical explanations that are offered for this potentially life-threatening disorder, and try to locate these within a wider context which takes account of the role and status of women in our society. In Chapter 9, we consider the problem of drug abuse among young people. We examine the social status of drug abuse in relation to other forms of addiction and the factors which maintain and escalate the problem for some individuals. The medical and legal frameworks are important influences upon the development of social work initiatives with drug abusers, and we consider the implications of this for liaison and co-operation in planning intervention.

Chapter 10 deals with the related problem of substance abuse. The problem of solvent abuse, in particular, has increased markedly in the last decade. Many professionals feel powerless to effect improvement for youngsters who are 'hooked' on potentially harmful substances. We consider the roles and responsibilities of parents and professionals in responding to the challenge of substance abuse.

The problem of suicidal behaviour among the young is an increasing one, and a cause for concern to many health and welfare professionals. In Chapter 11 we examine deliberate self-poisoning as the most common form of suicidal behaviour, and assess the knowledge we have gained from the growing research literature in this field. We consider vulnerability factors which make this harmful behaviour more available to some young people rather than others, and at the factors which precipitate a suicidal episode.

We end with a concluding chapter which seeks to underline the main themes within the book and a guide to further reading. This will, we hope, enable the interested reader to pursue in greater depth some of the ideas advanced elsewhere in this book.

We have had two main objectives in mind in writing this book. First, we wanted to provide an introductory text for CQSW and CSS students confronted by complex childhood and adolescent problems. This is a vast field, and we have been selective in our choice of topics, having in mind the complementary books in this series. We have written about these problems with the generic social worker, or residential officer in mind. It is our belief that too many social workers shy away from problems that they perceive to be either intractible, overly complicated, or best left to some form of specialist. This belief has grown from our work in both supervising and training basic grade workers. It follows, therefore, that the book will also be of interest to training officers, supervisors, and managers.

Our second aim has been to attempt to bridge the gap between the generic social worker, and those who work in specialist child or adolescent settings. A great deal of knowledge and skill has been built up in these specialist agencies and we believe that this could be shared more widely throughout the social work profession.

2

Childhood Problems – The Social Work Context

Family difficulties have always loomed large on the social work agenda, and many of the children involved are likely to have emotional, developmental, or behavioural difficulties. Indeed, much of social work activity is concerned either directly, or indirectly, with the needs of children. Children who are exhibiting problem behaviour at home, for example, may find their parent(s) seeking direct help for this. Alternatively, the request may come indirectly to social work via a third party, such as a health visitor or school nurse. Such problem behaviour in children may, however, form only a part of a broader and more complex pattern of problems. For example, the referral for social work help may be for direct intervention in the parents' relationship difficulties, or the practical problems of bad housing, poor health, low income, or debt management. The child's problems may go unnoticed, or be accorded little priority amid other more pressing problems.

The setting in which problems occur will influence the route of referral and the ultimate destination. Problems occurring within the school setting, for example, may well be dealt with by an educational psychologist, and education welfare officer, or may be referred to social workers within a child guidance centre via an educational psychologist. Alternatively, problems which come to light during a routine health examination in school, may be referred to a hospital-based child psychiatry service by the school medical officer. Referrals for help may take a similar 'medical' route if identified by health visitors. Recently, the concern about child abuse has resulted in greater awareness, and improved liaison between health visitors and social workers. In some cases this has meant an improvement in the referral process between the two agencies.

Once a referral has been made, the child's problem may soon take on a much wider dimension as family, school, peer group, and the Law (among others) become drawn into a spiral of response and counter-response. The manifestations of the problem may then appear as exclusion from school, parental rejection, non-accidental injury, or a court appearance, In turn, a number of agencies are likely to become involved. The social worker's task includes being aware of what the medical, health visiting, school psychological, educational, and voluntary agencies may have to contribute, as well as when and how to refer to them.

Social work services

Social work with children occurs in a variety of settings, and the development of services in relation to children with problems has been diverse and uneven. Child care teams within Social Services have traditionally been associated with issues of care, protection, and control of children, and with substitute parenting. Because of its medical connotations, 'treatment' of childrens' problems was more commonly associated with units within hospitals, and clinics. The 'medicalising' of problems followed from the fact that, whilst lip-service was paid to the concept of multi-disciplinary teams, invariably doctors stood at the top of the staffing hierarchy. As they were seen to carry overall clinical responsibility for the service, their voice was the dominant one.

The organisation of these services began to change with the creation of Social Departments (SSDs) in the early 1970s. The change arose from the need to impose a clear system of line-management upon social workers in peripheral (peripatetic) hospital or clinic settings. A second, though later force for change, has been the move within many SSDs to promote community-based services for a variety of groups, and to move away from services which are associated with institutions, or more 'isolated' settings. These practical changes have resulted in important shifts of emphasis within the service.

The organisation of services between institutions and the community created a number of difficulties for social workers in these different settings. An artifical divide had built up over the years between those social workers who worked within medically-oriented settings, and those based in community teams. The hospital- or clinic-based social work services acquired for themselves a mystique of 'specialism', operating as they did within the aura of medicine. Their 'specialism' might refer to the type of problems dealt with by the agency, or to the particular client group upon whom their therapeutic efforts were focused. The social workers within these settings had access to skills, knowledge, and resources (via doctors) which were not perceived as being available to social workers with the community-based services. Social workers in area teams, however, often saw themselves as having far greater professional independence than their clinically-based colleagues, and a greater access to resources controlled by the SSD. However, because of the generic nature of caseloads, it was often difficult for these social workers to pursue special interests. Statutory obligations, particularly with regard to child care, often dominated their professional agendas.

In our view, these apparent 'differences' between the two sectors have been exaggerated. In many parts of the country the past five years has seen greater harmony developing, and a greater integration of ideas for the development of services. Clinically-based social workers have increasingly become involved with statutory duties, hitherto the province of their area-based colleagues. They have also broadened their role in relation to work within the community so that follow-up services to clients discharged from hospital care are provided from the hospital, as well as the community-based agencies. There is greater liaison and interchange of ideas between social workers in different settings, so that each has a greater understanding of the roles and responsibilities of the other. In like manner, social workers from area teams work jointly with hospital personnel in their client's interests, thus preserving a valuable continuity of professional care.

Alongside these structural changes, which have resulted in hospital- and clinic-based social workers becoming more closely identified with mainstream social work, have gone important developments in social work technique. Social workers have played a major part in championing the development of family therapy, for example. Initially, family therapy was confined to clinical settings but its value is increasingly becoming recognised by workers in area teams. Some have applied these skills to situations of family crisis where children are about to come into care, and where there are difficulties or disruptions in fostering. Social workers are then increasingly working across professional and bureaucratic boundaries, and becoming more willing to share their skills.

The social work role

The social work task with children and adolescents is, in our view, essentially the following: assessment; therapeutic intervention; liaison with other agencies; the protection of children subject to abuse or neglect; advice and counselling in cases of matrimonial difficulty; and the provision of alternative carers should this become necessary. Many of these tasks are shared with other professionals, so an ability to liaise and appropriately refer on to other agencies is essential.

Assessment can be regarded as a prerequisite of any planned social work intervention, whatever its focus and scope. It is quite evident that a social worker will need to obtain a variety of information regarding a problem, perhaps from diverse sources, in order to formulate a response to it. In the case of childhood and adolescent problems, part of the social work assessment will usually focus upon the child's developmental history, family structure and relationships, and environmental factors. In this, the social worker utilises knowledge gained from developmental psychology, social psychology, sociology, and social policy and administration. But the social worker will also attend to issues specific to the referred problem. In the case of a child referred, for example, with a school-attendance problem, the social worker will pay particular attention to school factors in the child's and the family's history. The family's attitude to school attendance, the value placed on education within the family, and the quality of the parents' relationship with school personnel are all factors important to an understanding of the child's difficulties. Planned intervention by social workers in the problems of children and adolescents utilises skills which are available within a wide variety of the 'helping' professions. In summary, these are:

1. Individual casework/psychotherapy

Broadly this falls into the two categories of (a) supportive, and (b) interpretive. Supportive work with a parent or parents will often help them through a difficult period with a child. In many of these cases the parents are often making valient efforts to cope with a very difficult and demanding child, but doubt their capacity to manage this, and begin to lose confidence. Supportive work offers them encouragement and reassurance with regard to their own parenting skills, and an opportunity to express their frustration, disappointment, and anger in a safe neutral setting.

Interpretive work is much more akin to individual psychotherapy, in that it aims to help parents to understand why things are the way they are. By making links between current stresses and individual functioning, the social worker promotes an awareness of the relationship between past events, their impact, and their continuing influence upon current functioning. Making sense of the past, and recognising its persistence into the present, can be of immense value to parents in motivating them towards new and more rewarding styles of interaction with their children.

Individual work with children has traditionally been the province of child psychiatrists, but in recent years greater professional flexibility has brought both psychologists and social workers into this area of work. Play is the natural medium of the child and various techniques using art materials, dolls, etc., have been developed. The medium of play can be extremely useful in helping children to express feelings and opinions which would normally remain hidden. With older children and adolescents, simple psychotherapy can be used to explore issues which are causing them difficulty at home.

2. Behaviour therapy

Behaviour therapy utilises learning theory in the development of specific treatment plans which are usually time limited. Unlike psychotherapy, behaviour therapy focusses very much on current problems and the capacity and motivation for change. The first stage in offering this kind off treatment intervention is to identify the behaviour which is to be the focus for change, and to monitor the regularity and intensity of its occurrence. From this 'baseline' data a systematic programme of activity and observation can be instituted, using small rewards for effort and achievement

Other behavioural techniques can be used to help parents achieve greater consistency and co-operation in their management of the child. They can be taught to monitor their own reactions to provocative behaviour in a child, and to be more selective in their responses. Often this will simply involve praising and rewarding good behaviour, ignoring bad behaviour, or perhaps diverting the child into some more positive activity. Parents may use brief 'time-out' periods to deal with particularly disruptive and provocative episodes.

3. Marital therapy

Clearly, many children's problems are caused, or are made worse by continuing friction between the parents. Direct work with parents may be aimed at helping them through a difficult or stressful period in their relationship, or it may address itself to major longstanding difficulties in the marriage. Where parental differences are irreconcilable, then the social work task may be one of conciliation between the partners as they move towards separation or divorce.

4. Family therapy

In recent years, family therapy has grown in popularity among a number of the helping professions as an important method of intervention. A number of different models have been developed. All of these aim, either implicitly or explicitly, to explore functioning within the family group, to understand the emotional interaction between family members, their problem-solving skills, and the overall rules by which the family attempts to order its experiences. Family therapy often involves the use of two therapists either working together in the room, or with one therapist observing the work of the other via a one-way screen. The work is usually short-term and is often based around a contract agreed between the family and the therapist(s).

5. *Group therapy*

Young people often benefit from being part of a group, and social workers are both knowledgeable and familiar with this form of intervention. Groups can be educative, supportive, or problem-solving, or may combine elements of all these functions. Social skills groups for young people have an important educative function in helping them to anticipate social situations, and to learn the skills necessary to manage these with confidence. Groups composed of children with similar difficultuies can be useful in promoting problem-solving skills, and in supporting individuals who are vulnerable. Group therapy may also extend to parents in order to offer them the support of a shared experience with other parents, and to promote the exchange of attitudes and opinions regarding parent-child functioning.

Knowledge and skill

What is expected from social workers in terms of knowledge and skill, in order effectively to assess and intervene in childhood problems? Generally, we would expect social workers to be knowledgeable about individual human development, and the internal and external influences upon this process. This will take account of biological, psychological, social and cultural issues in development.

Knowledge gained in these areas gives the social worker an overview of what may be considered both normal and abnormal in development. In biological development, abnormality may be identified because of visible external indicators in physical appearance (for example, failure to thrive in an infant). Abnormal features of psychological or social development would be more difficult to identify since these would be observed through behaviour within the family, or in some other social group, such as the classroom. Often the presence of a 'difficulty' must be deduced from behavioural cues, and from the context in which it occurs.

The following areas are, therefore, of importance to the social worker who wishes to have a role in the assessment and management of problems in children:

(a) a knowledge of 'normal' development in children, and ability to help parents understand this in relation to their own children. Knowledge of children who have special needs or problems, and helping parents and others to recognise the importance of the family in both causation and treatment;

(b) an understanding of the common stresses of childhood and adolescence, and the transition into adulthood;

(c) understanding the parenting task and its responsibilities. Understanding the demands this makes upon couples, and individuals, and the role of fact and fantasy in shaping their attitudes, opinions, and expectations. Knowledge of common parental anxieties, the difficulties they must negotiate, and the adverse consequences (for example, hostility, rejection, and abuse) that may arise from parenting failure;

(d) understanding adverse influences upon parenting, the personal and relationship difficulties which may preoccupy parents and divert them from parental responsibilities. The practical stresses of material hardship, unemployments, ill health, etc., and the emotional stresses of marital breakdown, loss, and bereavement;

(e) social workers have to know about and successfully interact with the network of national and local services available to help families and children;

(f) the statutory framework within which both the client and the professional services exist;

(g) social workers need to know how to work with individuals, dyads, and whole families;

(h) social workers need to be able to talk to children.

We would see this knowledge and skill as integral to an understanding of disturbance in children and their families. Possession of this provides a background from which to consider the more specific manifestations of disturbance, and their causativce factors. This is by no means a clearly defined area. Rather it can resemble a minefield of half-truths, contradictions, argument, and counter-argument. In the following chapters we have, therefore, endeavoured to keep 'technical' language to a minimum, to present the various arguments in a concise way, to draw upon our experience as lecturers, supervisors, and social work practitioners in order to promote the integration of theory and practice.

3
Eating and Sleeping Problems

Introduction

Childhood development is an area which contains a good deal of scope for the genesis of problems, and is something about which many parents experience a high degree of anxiety. Every day, parents (particularly mothers) are reminded of what is supposedly 'normal' in childhood development, either via popular magazines, television, and radio, or by direct contact with other mothers and their children. Comparisons are inevitable between both parents and their own children, and those of other people, and gradually an awareness of differences in development may grow which in turn may provoke parental anxiety. Many of these differences in maturation may simply reflect the normal variations which occur among children regarding ages and stages in development, but others will indicate a more specific delay which may be problematical. There are then two dimensions to developmental problems. The first is the parental reaction, which may not be a reflection of a legitimate problem, but which has to be responded to regardless of its cause. The second is the rate at which the child matures which, similarly, may constitute a genuine problem, or one which will in time resolve itself. The art lies in being able to respond sympathetically to both parents, and child, regardless of the ultimate cause of their concern.

In this chapter, we deal with two areas in which problems commonly occur: eating and sleeping. Developmental problems such as these can manifest themselves in a variety of

14

settings such as home, nursery or school, and also in residential establishments. GPs and health visitors frequently receive direct requests from parents for help or advice, but the problems may also present in rather more indirect ways. For example, some instances of child abuse may be associated with developmental problems. Not infrequently, the additional stress on the parents engendered by having to cope with a developmental difficulty may result in parental anger, or even violence, towards the child concerned, or to another sibling. Similarly, parents who consult their family doctor or outpatient psychiatric services with feelings of irritability, anxiety, or depression, may well be coping inadequately with a troublesome infant. Where there are other children in the family, all of whom are competing for parental time and energy, then the problem may present as a request to the SSD for temporary 'respite' Care. The developmental problems of one child can begin to generalise into other areas of behaviour, and into different environments.

EATING

Eating problems are very common in young children, and can sometimes arise in the absence of other significant difficulties. They are a rich source of anxiety for parents since a great deal of emphasis is placed upon the importance of correct diet for healthy development. Moreover, parents may still equate the rejection of food with a rejection of love and so react adversely to what they perceive as a criticism by the child, of themselves, and the quality of their parenting. In many ways this has grown more acute in recent years since much of the information available to parents through the media, and through bodies such as the Health Education Council, acts as a constant reminder that problems in later life, for example obesity, often have their roots in early childhood and the dietary regime established during that period.

Eating problems in childhood are usually categorised in the following ways:

● quantity of food intake – too little or too much;

- type of food – a balanced diet, or one which reflects 'food fads';
- Children who eat items which are not usually regarded as food.

One common eating problem is food refusal. Here, pressure from parents for children to eat certain quantities or types of food leads to resistance on the part of the child. Parental anxieties may stem from a natural worry that the child is not eating normally, when compared with other children. Alternatively, the parents may be quite rigid in their own eating habits, following a fairly strict regime which then puts pressure upon the child to conform. Some parents have what we might call 'The Clean Plate Syndrome' where the child is threatened with all manner of sanctions, or coerced, into finishing every item of food put before him. Mealtimes may well become a battle-ground, with neither side being prepared to capitulate nor compromise. In many cases the child will have eaten sufficient for his dietary requirements without finishing all that is placed before them. However, the parents may still insist on a clean plate, since this is what they believe to be 'correct'. In reality these children may be well-nourished and appear unconcerned about their meals or their food intake.

At the other end of the continuum are those children who not only eat their meals, but much else besides. Mealtimes are merely 'islands' in the sea of continuous eating. Such children will persistently complain of hunger, even after a large meal, and will supplement their meals with a variety of other sources of food. Again, this may create serious friction between the parents and child. This occurs not only because they may see an implicit accusation of 'starvation' levelled at them by their child's behaviour, but also because of the cost. This is a particular problem in families on limited incomes, when the cost of satisfying a voracious appetite with expensive 'snack' foods, proves burdensome.

Food fads

Faddiness in eating habits is very common among children who are food refusers. This may mean that only a very narrow range of foods are acceptable to the child. Again, there is usually marked parental anxiety even though the child is generally well-nourished and apparently unconcerned about their diet.

Pica

Pica refers to the eating of items which are not usually regarded as food, for example wood, paper, soil, fabrics. The condition is thought by some authorities to be indicative of environmental and emotional distress, and so may be an important indicator for the social worker to be aware of. It is also thought to be associated with distorted developmental patterns, brain damage, and mental retardation. The condition may also occur in children with normal mental development and is then usually associated with iron-deficiency anaemia and poor diet. Treatment of this potentially damaging situation may involve hospital admission because such children tend to come from extremely disorganised or disrupted families. In such cases a brief hospitalisation may be the only practicable step in the short term. Following this, intensive social work intervention focussing upon the usually extensive practical and emotional difficulties that the family face, is usually required.

Prevalence

Richman *et al.* (1973) studied the prevalence of a number of different behaviours, in a random sample of 3-year-old London children, and found that about 13 per cent were reported to have food fads.

Theoretical models

Because eating problems tend to manifest themselves in the context of covert or overt pressure from parents, this is usually taken as the starting point for any explanatory model. Put at its simplest, the parents, it is believed, exert pressure upon the child. The child then *selects* a symptom which is likely to exacerbate parental anxiety. Gradually a system develops in which increased parental anxiety leads in turn to an increase in the troublesome symptom and so on. Both parties then become locked into a battle which neither can win.

Family influences

A number of factors may contribute to the initial feelings of anxiety or inadequacy on the part of parents. Some parents may be young and inexperienced in their handling of children. Others may have experienced inconsistent or uncaring attitudes from their own parents in the past which has, therefore, given them little confidence in their own parenting skills. In a small number of cases the parents' own childhood may have been disrupted by family breakdown, or even exposure to unsympathetic institutional regimes and periods 'in Care'. Parents may be ignorant of the normal dietary requiremens of children, particularly very young children, and be providing food which is inappropriate, or which the child simply cannot manage at his age and developmenal stage. Relatives too, may induce anxiety, particularly their own parents, by critically commenting upon the child's physical stature, poor growth, inadequate table manners, etc. This may be exacerbated by the fact that, not infrequently, the child appears to eat 'normally' when away from home.

Management

In addition to taking a full developmental and social history from the parents, it is often useful for social workers to encourage the parents to keep a diary of what the child actually eats at home, and, if appropriate, at nursery, or school. This will enable them to construct a 'baseline' of the child's eating habits, and will be particularly useful if a behavioural method of intervention is subsequently used in treatment.

Work with the parents can be both educative and therapeutic. Where the child is temperamentally difficult and the parents are basically trying to follow a sensible and appropriate plan of management, then social work support may be necessary to sustain them in this. They may well appreciate the opportunity of having an 'outsider' to discuss the problem with, rather than family or friends, and this reassurance, and the opportunity to ventilate their feelings, may be sufficient in itself. Intervention may mean direct involvement with the social worker, or alternatively, the social worker acting as a resource person who can, for example, put parents in touch with local parents' groups.

Whatever the type of intervention decided upon, there are two points which the social worker will need to remind the parents of in their daily management. Firstly, insofar as it is possible, the parents should ignore the symptom and resist becoming involved in mealtime friction. The social worker would be useful here in suggesting various 'diversionary tactics' which the parents might employ to avoid a confrontation. For example, the parents could allow the child to have a particular toy with them at table, or turn the meal into a game with small treats for those who finish the meal. The parents would need to start by giving the child small amounts of food at mealtimes, and gradually increase this as progress is made. Secondly, the parents should avoid becoming caught in the trap of preparing special meals for the child, either to suit his whims, or to tempt him to eat more. Parents who do this are on a 'hiding to nothing' since this will place the child in a superior, and quite inappropriate position of power.

The current emphasis in health literature and the media about food additives has not only increased public awareness about the issue, but has also increased parental anxieties. Many eating difficulties, and other problematic behaviours are now attributed by parents to a food allergy syndrome. Consequently, medical investigation may be sought by anxious parents in an attempt to establish a biological cause for their child's difficult behaviour. While some children clearly do have specific food allergies which affect their physical and emotional well-being, others may be defined in this way by parents to avoid facing up to and takling what is basically a behaviour-management problem between parents and child.

Outcome

For many toddlers, eating problems represent a phase in their development which is an integral part of their need to assert themselves, and to rebel against parental authority. Children have many ways of testing parental resolve, and limits to behaviour, and eating may be just one feature of this process. The outcome for such children is usually good. However, where parental attitudes are negative and intransigent, the problem may persist into later childhood. In such cases, the eating disorder may well act as the vehicle for much more serious family disturbance, which might have very little to do with the child and his eating problem.

Summary points

- Eating problems in children are common, particularly among younger children.
- They are often related to parental anxieties about the child's eating habits, or more generalised anxieties regarding the child's overall development, and the responsibilities of parenting.
- In younger parents the problem may stem from ignorance or unfamiliarity with age appropriate behaviours or developmental norms.
- Children usually obtain sufficient nourishment in spite of their erratic or irregular eating habits.
- The more difficult problem of Pica often arises in disorganised families, and may result in neurological damage or impairment.

* * *

Anna, aged 4, was referred because of slowness in eating, and food refusal. Parental fears that she was undernourished had previously led to referral to a paediatrician. The parents had been reassured by this since medical investigation revealed that her weight and height were within the norms for her age. The eating problem had continued, however, and the parents became irritated and frustrated at the lack of improvement. Both of Anna's parents were in full-time employment and she attended a nursery in the mornings, and was cared for by a child minder in the afternoons. Her main contact with her parents was, therefore, at meal times and bedtime. Weekends were also busy, in that father was making extensive improvements to the home, and mother was preoccupied by shopping and household chores which had accumulated during the working week.

By encouraging the parents to keep a diary of their daily activities at home, a number of suggestions were made which would restructure their time and allow them more direct contact with Anna. Examples of these were:

- Father spending time on a weekday evening playing with Anna or reading to her, while mother went late-night shopping:
- arranging a regular time each week when Anna would have a friend to visit for tea, and play. This would have the additionals benefit of ensuring that Anna would receive similar invitations from other children:
- introducing more flexibility into mealtimes, for example small amounts of food for Anna; more time to eat it; allowing her to have a favourite doll or cuddly toy at table to 'eat' with her:
- involving Anna in positive food experiences, for example being allowed to choose occasional 'treats' for her meals; helping mother to prepare a meal (washing vegetables, rolling out pastry, etc.) and being praised for this.

As many of the suggestions involved the rethinking of how parents used their time, improvement was initially slow, but with encouragement and support they were able to persevere and achieve the goals that had been established with the social worker in their initial contract.

*　　　*　　　*

SLEEP PROBLEMS

Sleep is another area, like eating, in which there may be considerable variation as to what constitutes a norm in terms of a child's developmental needs. Sleep problems may arise, therefore, where parents are unaware of the appropriate norms, or lacking in the basic knowledge of child development. They are also common in disorganised homes where there is a lack of consistency over bedtimes, and where the parents and children do not have a routine for this part of the day. A varied sleep pattern, which may be perceived as a problem by parents, is common among very young babies. This will normally resolve itself if regular routines are maintained and no other significant problems exist in the family.

The most common presentation of sleep problems in the very young child is night-waking and the difficulties associated with settling the infant back to sleep. Physical and emotional factors will be important here, as will the individual temperament of the child. The child may wake through physical discomfort, caused by hunger, or a wet or soiled nappy. Similarly, teething, colic, and other physical ailments are likely to produce disturbed nights for both child and parents.

Toddlers, and even tiny babies, are sensitive to variations in the emotional atmosphere at home, though parents may not readily appreciate this. Emotional strains will affect the parents' handling of the infant, and produce changes in their regular routine which the child will very probably become aware of.

The child's temperament will also influence their sleeping behaviour. Some children are more active than others, they require less sleep, are more irregular in their habits, and slow to establish a pattern to their sleeping and other behaviours. Such children are often more demanding of their parents since the irregularity and unpredictability of sleeping habits will demand more involvement from the parents and allow them less time to themselves.

Other types of sleep problem, such as nightmares and night terrors, can be more alarming in their presentation.

Nightmares

Nightmares are vivid and frightening dreams which occur in association with rapid eye movement (REM) sleep. The child does not usually awaken during a nightmare, but it he does so, then he is likely to behave quite normally. Many children have occasional nightmares and the experience is frequently linked to some fear or anxiety that the child has. This is not usually regarded as a problem unless the nightmares are occurring regularly.

Night terrors

Night terrors occur on waking from deep sleep and are

associated with dream content. Children having night terrors will present as disorientated, or even hallucinated, talking to imaginary beings, and unaware of the parent's presence in the bedroom. This can be very disturbing for parents who have not witnessed such episodes before, particularly as the child's trance-like state renders him unresponsive to the parents attempts to comfort him. Night terrors can last for periods of up to 15 minutes, sometimes longer, and the child will usually settle back to sleep without difficulty once this is over. It is not usual for the child to recollect the episode the following morning.

Sleep walking

Night terrors and nightmares may be accompanied by sleep walking in children. The content of the 'terror' or nightmare is acted out by the child in a state of sleep or altered consciousness. Again, the child is unlikely to recollect the sleep walking episode the following day.

Sometimes sleep disturbance is associated with physical disorders, for example influenza, when the child may have a raised temperature. A small proportion of children may need more specialised investigation by a neurologist, if their continued sleep disturbance seems to indicate more serious difficulties such as night-time epiletic seizures. It follows that any continuing sleep disturbance should be discussed with the family doctor at an early stage, to ensure that appropriate specialist advice is obtained.

In the absence of other significant problems, sleep disorder can be regarded as a common and transient feature of development during infancy. Where there is evidence of emotional disorder in the child or family, then the sleep problem may well persist.

Prevalence

Richman (1981) estimates that 1 in 5 pre-school children will present with a major and persisting sleep problem. Furthermore, she maintains that between a half and three-quarters of young children will experience periods of poor sleep at some time. Moreover, all young babies will have night-time episodes of crying, for which no amount of consolation seems sufficient to sooth them. Armed with such information a social worker may well be able to reassure an anxious parent who is concerned about their child's sleep.

Management

The management of sleep problems in children is geared towards establishing a routine which clearly emphasises the difference between daytime and nightime activities, and where the routine for the latter is followed with firmness and consistency. Specific interventions will usually employ behavioural techniques in problem management and, therefore, the initial task will be to obtain from the parents a baseline record or diary of nightime activities and routine. A record which has been kept by parents will give a clear picture of what the problems are, when they occur, and with what regularity.

The next step is to obtain agreement with the parents regarding the specific changes they wish to see, and to follow this with some discussion of the techniques to be used. It is important for the social worker to determine early on whether or not this will be a shared responsibility between both partners. Unless both parents are willing to invest time and energy (and loss of sleep) in the treatment plan, then setbacks are very likely, and the chances of success limited. It is important that the parents present a firm and united front to the child. If this is lacking, the child may doubt the veracity of the parents' statements and actions. Moreover, any divisions between the parents will be exposed and exploited. This unity of purpose may be particularly difficult to sustain if, as is frequently the case, lack of sleep is leaving them feeling tired, irritable, and emotionally and physically drained.

Once there are agreed goals, then a management programme can be worked out between the parents and the social worker. For example, where the child wakes several times during the night, the parents can adopt a regime for checking and soothing the child which is appropriate to them, but which minimises the likelihood of the child feeling rewarded for this behaviour. Settling the child with firmness, but without undue cuddling or concern, will establish a different routine to which the child may quickly adapt.

Where children frequently end up sleeping in the parents' bed, a firm routine of returning the child to his own bed, perhaps using small rewards to encourage the child to stay there, is likely to lead to success. Where the child is older, and better able to understand his parents' concerns, then he may more easily respond to a programme linked to a reward system, whereby he can participate in keeping a diary or a merit chart.

In the assessment stage of problem-management, some liaison will be necessary if other professionals are involved in the care of the family, The parents may already be receiving advice from their GP or health visitor, and contact with these services will be essential in order to avoid duplication of effort, or the giving of conflicting advice.

Parents will need ongoing support and reassurance if their motivation is to be sustained, since persistent sleep disturbance in a child can be a highly disruptive influence in their lives. They may not realise that their problem is an extremely common one, particularly with younger children, and that they are not alone in seeking help and advice in its management. Frequently, what is perceived as a problem by a parent diminishes, if put into a broader perspective. Reassurance which stresses the fact that many children act in the way being described by the parent, not infrequently dissipates the concern.

Summary points

- Sleep disturbance in early childhood is common and is usually a transient problem.
- Physical, emotional, and temperamental factors are important in the causation of the disturbance, and factors which adversely affect parental handling will also have significance.

- Sleep disturbance is more likely to occur at stressful periods in the child's life (e.g. starting school).
- Night terrors and sleep walking have a much more physiological basis to them. They occur when part of the brain is in an aroused state while the rest of the brain is still in deep sleep.
- In general, sleep problems in children will respond to sympathetic but firm and consistent handling by parents.

*   *   *

Craig, aged 4, began to wake in the night for no apparent reason, and was difficult to get back to sleep. He had recently started school, appeared to have adapted well, but began to complain that he had no friends. Many of his friends had started school a term earlier than Craig, and had already become established within their peer group.

Social work support was offered to the parents to help them manage this difficulty. They were encouraged to be patient in their night-time handling, and intially to allow Craig into their own bed to help him relax. The parents accepted the suggestion that they should discuss the problem with Craig's class teacher, so that she could help in promoting his peer group relationships in school. The teacher was able to arrange for Craig, and two other children, to jointly carry out small tasks for her on a regular basis. The social worker suggested that the parents might consolidate the teacher's efforts by getting Craig to invite these children home after school. As the term progressed, the teacher was able to help Craig to extend his circle of friendships. By the end of term he had settled back into a normal sleep pattern.

*   *   *

Jane began to have night terrors at age 10, while staying in a Social Services pre-fostering placement. The night-staff often found her crouched upon her bed, shouting and screaming, but seemingly unaware of their presence in the bedroom.

Jane's early life had been unsettled and difficult. She was conceived by her mother at 16 as a result of a casual liaison with a local youth. Jane was raised by her maternal grandmother, her own mother having married when Jane was 3, moving with her husband to another town. The grandmother's household was a turbulent one in which grandmother and her two unmarried children often argued and verbally abused one another. Jane became increasingly involved in these arguments and suffered some physical abuse as a result. Her relatives soon began to regard her as uncontrollable and, following a number of occasions when Jane had been missing from home, she was received into Care.

The appearance of night terrors coincided with preliminary visits Jane had made with her social worker to some prospective foster parents. Not unexpectedly, Jane was anxious about her future and the prospect of becoming part of another family. Her past experiences of family life had made her pessimistic about coping with a 'new' family, and with their expectations of her.

Jane's social worker joined with the Care staff in producing a management plan for her night-time disturbances. This involved spending a little time each day with Jane, to discuss her past experiences and to help her to make sense of these. The aim was to build up her self-esteem so that with continuing support, she would be better able to face the future. A member of night-staff also gave Jane some individual time at bedtime, talking about the day's happenings or reading a story to her, before she went to sleep. During the ensuing weeks Jane's night terrors decreased, and this joint work was carried forward into her foster placement.

4

Some Problems of Toileting

Introduction

Bladder and bowel habits in children vary considerably, particularly during the early years, and can be a source of acute and continuing anxiety for parents. The failure to achieve bladder or bowel control in accordance with developmental norms may reflect, in some children, a maturational delay, but in others it may be indicative of more serious disturbance. Perhaps more frequent than either of these two situations is that in which a parent becomes concerned about a child's failure to achieve what may be quite unrealistic parental expectations.

ENURESIS

Nocturnal enuresis (bedwetting) is the most common presentation of this problem, and often occurs on its own. Diurnal enuresis (daytime wetting) is less common but can accompany nocturnal enuresis, and is less likely to occur on its own. Children normally achieve bladder continence between 3 and 4 years of age, and incontinence of urine after the age of 5 is considered abnormal. As with other forms of developmental disorder in children, parents may cope with the problem for some time without reference to any specialist services, so that when the child is referred for help, the problem may have become well-established. Enuresis is usually divided into primary and secondary. Primary enuresis refers to those

28

children who have never achieved bladder control, while secondary enuresis includes those children who, having achieved bladder control for a time, then begin to wet again.

Prevalence

Nocturnal enuresis is a common problem which decreases with age. At age 5 the incidence is approximately 10 per cent, falling to 5 per cent at age 10, and 2 per cent from 10 years onwards. The rates may be culture-specific since cultural variations in child-rearing practices will produce different rates at different ages (e.g. rates in the USA are higher than for the UK). The rates for diurnal enuresis are lower, only 2 per cent of children at age 5 having this problem. Between the ages of 4 and 6 wetting is common in both boys and girls. After the age of 7 years, however, the rate for boys increases so that by age 11, there are twice as many boys as girls. Enuresis commonly runs in families, and one study found that approximately 70 per cent of all enuretics have a first-degree relative who is, or has been enuretic (Bakwin, 1961).

Theoretical models

Opinion regarding enuresis is by no means clear-cut, and a number of explanations exist. For example, the fact that enuretic children often have a family history of this problem suggests that there is a genetic component to the disorder. Findings from other studies of children have suggested that:

- enuresis is not usually indicative of physical abnormality, though some children may have small bladder capacity and will pass urine more frequently than others. In girls, enuresis is associated with infections of the urinary tract and occasionally there is a structural abnormality present in the tract;
- enuresis is also linked with certain physical problems such as nocturnal epilepsy, and diabetes;
- enuresis is regarded by some as an indication of emotional

disorders in children. This may present as 'regression', when the child is thought to be reverting to a form of behaviour associated with a much earlier stage in development, or it may be a symptom of a developing neurotic disorder;

● it has been suggested that the period between 1½ and 4½ years is a 'sensitive' period for the learning of bladder control. Adverse life events occurring during this time may, therefore, disrupt the acquisition of control;

● some children may experience a delay in the maturation of the nervous system which will result in enuresis;

● delayed bladder control is a feature of children who have a mental handicap.

Enuresis appears to be more frequent in children of low social class or living in crowded or disadvantages circumstances, and among those children reared in institutions (Essen & Peckham, 1976).

Management

Social workers who are involved in work with families are well-used to hearing complaints from parents about bedwetting in their children. Special considerations in the assessment of an enuretic child and his family would relate to the duration and regularity of the Enuresis, and to the attitudes of other family members and peers. Systematic reporting by the parents is important especially as behaviour modification is likely to be the treatment of choice. It is also essential to note the child's toileting habits both at home and in school, and the situational response to these. The attitude of other family members is an important consideration since a negative or punitive reaction may well exacerbate the problem by producing shame, embarrassment, or guilt in the child. The enuresis may adversely affect the child's social functioning and limit his involvement in certain social activities such as spending the night away from home on school trips, or overnight camp with Cubs or Scouts. Assessment of the social characteristics of the problem, and the context(s) in which it occurs will help establish the child's level of competency in coping with the problem, as well as in other areas of his life.

Once organic factors have been excluded, the treatment of enuresis will often involve the use of behavioural techniques. All behavioural approaches begin by identifying a specific 'target' behaviour, followed by a detailed record (baseline chart) of the frequency and intensity of the behaviour. The child can assist in drawing up a baseline record of his enuresis, possibly using a merit chart on which he can award himself stars for his achievements. Younger children are likely to respond positively to the use of a 'star chart', particularly if it is eye-catching and imaginative in design. The chart may be combined with the use of an enuresis alarm which is designed to waken the child from sleep so that he may then go to the lavatory. The alarm is also known as a 'bell and pad' since a wired pad is placed beneath the draw-sheet on which the child will lie, and this is then connected to a small alarm (a bell or buzzer). When drops of urine come into contact with the pad this activates the alarm which then wakes the child. The use of behavioural techniques, however, demand quite a high level of motivation in both the child and the other family members, if they are to be successful. Success rates of up to 80 per cent have been reported in families where the enuresis alarm has been properly used and monitored. Adopting this approach would prove less successful if it were to be introduced into a disorganised family, or one in which a number of other stresses such as overcrowding, material disadvantage, and financial pressures were present. In such cases the parents' capacity to respond effectively may be limited by their need to cope with other pressing problems.

For some largely-unexplained reason, anti-depresent drugs, such as Imipramine, have proved an effective medication for nocturnal enuresis. However, they do not appear to be the answer in the long-term. Doctors are naturally reluctant to use such medication on small children, and relapses are common. It may, however, be an effective way of coping with the problem in the short-term. For example, in enabling a child to spend a couple of nights away from home on a school trip: something which, if the bedwetting were to continue, would prove socially embarrassing for the child concerned.

Social work with the parents will aim at reassuring them about the condition and its prognosis. It should be explained to parents that enuresis is a common problem which is best seen in terms of a delay in learning bladder control. For parents who have a tendency to react in a negative way to the problem, it should be emphasised that the wetting is involuntary and not, therefore, a deliberate action in the part of the child. Practical measures in which the parents could become involved would include restricting the child's fluid intake in the evenings, and lifting the child from bed during the night in order to take him to the lavatory. Parents can also encourage the child to become accustomed to the sensation of having a full bladder by getting him to delay his visits to the lavatory for increasingly longer periods. These measures demand patience and persistence from parents, and some sacrifice in terms of disrupting their own regular sleeping habits in order to attend to their child. However, if they can be adhered to by the parties concerned, then there can often be quite dramatic improvements. Some authors do not support such practical measures by parents. They argue that these may in fact inhibit the acquisition of bladder control, because they disrupt the overall maturational process. Nevertheless, many parents will continue these practices in order to support their child's efforts, particularly where such methods have achieved some degree of success in the past.

Outcome

Children tend to grow out of their enuresis problem. In the 6 to 9 years age group good results have been reported following the use of a bell and pad, but this is less so for older children. Improvement is less likely in children from impoverished or disorganised homes, where treatment plans are difficult to pursue, or where other emotional problems intervene. It should be recognised that where the problem of Enuresis is chronic, then the child may need in-patient assessment and treatment if he is to have the best change of overcoming the difficulty.

Summary points

- Enuresis which occurs, or continues, after age 5, is considered abnormal. Nocturnal enuresis is much more-common than diurnal.
- There is usually no association with physical abnormality in the child, though infections and structural abnormalities of the urinary tract are more likely to occur in girls than boys. Medical investigation will be necessary to exclude possible organic factors.
- Genetic factors may be important, as may physical problems such as diabetes or nocturnal epilepsy.
- Enuresis is associated with emotional problems, and with delays in maturation of the nervous system.
- Delayed bladder control is a feature of children who have a mental handicap.
- Behavioural methods of treatment are most common, utilising a merit chart and enuresis alarm. Drug treatment may occasionally be advocated.
- Regular and careful monitoring of behavioural programmes will be necessary, particularly with disorganised families. Practical advice on problem management, and on welfare benefit entitlement may be required to help families cope with the enuretic child at home.
- Chronic enuresis may respond to in-patient assessment and treatment by a child psychiatric team.

*   *   *

Tracy (7) came into Care because of parental rejection and physical neglect. She settled well into a Family Group Home, but her long standing problem of day and nightime wetting continued. The houseparents were helped to set up a programme in which Tracy was taken to the toilet at regular intervals, and liaison with her headteacher enabled this programme to be continued during school hours. The daytime wetting improved dramatically, but her night-time wetting continued unabated. A merit chart, using stars and small rewards, was introduced and an enuresis alarm was obtained for use in the evenings. The other children in the home were briefed as to its purpose, and were encouraged to praise Tracy for any achievements. An older boy in the home, who had himself been enuretic, became close to Tracy, and protective of her. She responded positively to this, and gradually the enuresis began to improve.

*   *   *

ENCOPRESIS

Children are normally clean and continent of faeces by the age of 3. Encopresis (faecal soiling) is considered abnormal after the age of 4. Commonly it involves the passing of faeces into clothing, e.g. underwear, pyjamas, etc., and may be accompanied by smearing.

Prevalence

Encopresis is much less common then enuresis, and is found more often in boys than in girls. General population studies give an overall prevalence rate at age 7 of 2.3 per cent for boys, and 0.7 per cent for girls. By age 11, the rate has fallen overall to 1.3 per cent for boys, and 0.3 per cent for girls (Bellman, 1966). Rutter *et al.* (1970) found a prevalence of once a month soiling of 1.3 per cent in boys, and 0.3 per cent in girls, among 12-year-olds in their Isle of Wight study.

Theoretical models

There have been many schemes of classification in the literature, emphasising variables such as constitutional factors in the child's bowel function, school factors, disturbed parent–child relationships and expectations regarding bowel training, and psychodynamic factors in the child. Hersov (1985) believes, however, that models of the causation of encopresis can best be understood by considering the three main ways in which the disorder usually presents.

(a) Primary encopresis

Children in this group have progressed from birth without ever gaining bowel control, and they are often enuretic as well. They tend to come from homes which often reflect little order or consistency in routine, and a good deal of social disadvantage. Many of these children have associated emotional problems or intellectual problems which have made school life difficult to cope with. Commonly these children will pass motions into their clothing.

(b) Secondary encopresis

Children with secondary encopresis usually begin soiling after a period during which they have achieved bowel control. It is often associated with wider emotional disturbance and the symptom may be regression on the child's part to an earlier, more dependent stage of development. Having previously been independent, the child may now exhibit excessive dependency by becoming 'clingy' and tearful with parents. This behaviour can often be precipitated by some emotional trauma such as the birth of a sibling, when the child may experience a withdrawal of parental attention from himself to the new baby, coupled with changed parental expectations of himself since he is no longer the 'baby' in the family. The child may become secretive about his soiling by hiding soiled underwear, or faeces, in inappropriate places around the house (for example, under the bed, or behind furniture). In addition to soiling themselves, these children may also smear faeces on to walls or furniture.

(c) Constipation with overflow soiling

When the problem presents in this way, it often reflects a disturbed relationship between the child and his primary caretaker (usually the mother). It can stem from toilet training which was begun too early, or where there has been pressure from parents to achieved bowel control as soon as possible. Such parents may be obsessional, or overly concerned about cleanliness and tidiness. Their fastidiousness may allow the child no opportunity for dirty or rough play, or the normal expression of aggressive or negativistic behaviour. The 'bowel' symptom is selected by the child because it is likely to be one to which the parent is extremely vulnerable. The soiling is often retentive in that the child may be constipated through his stubborn refusal to pass faeces. The soiling will occur through the overflow of more liquid faeces around the faecal blockage. This is likely to produce staining of clothing rather than the passage of full motions into the clothing. The child will, therefore, have added a physical complication to the problem, the large bowel often becoming distended through retention of faeces. Another physical problem is anal fissure, where a tear in the bowel lining produces pain on defaecation, and understandable reluctance on the part of the child to pass faeces. A relatively rare physical complication is Hirchsprung's Disease. This is a congenital condition which results in constipation and overflow because of an absence of physical sensation in a section of the colon. In other words, the internal signals which would normally indicate to a child the need to pass faeces do not occur.

Management

The form in which the encopresis presents will largely determine the form in which therapeutic intervention will be offered. It is important, therefore, to obtain a clear and accurate account of the soiling from the parents. Attention must obviously be given to any organic factors which are thought to be relevant, and the extent to which these have been subject to medical investigation. As parents will be closely involved in the treatment plans, it is important to explore family attitudes to the problem, and the extent to which these may be maintaining the problem in the child. In particular, those parents who are punitive towards the child, blaming him for what they see as dirty and embarrassing behaviour, are likely to escalate the emotional difficulties in the child. It is also important to assess the reactions of siblings and peers since they may well have incorporated negative parental attitudes towards the problem, and the child may be subject to a good deal of ridicule and ostracism both at home and in school.

Treatment will depend upon the age of the child, the way in which the problem presents, and on what is perceived to be the cause of the soiling. With primary encopresis, failure to provide normal toilet training may respond to a programme of firm and consistent training, and help for the parents in carrying this out. Efforts would also be directed at increasing the parents' sensitivity to the child's difficulties. These measures may need to be undertaken in a residential setting, though a home-based treatment programme may be possible in some cases. However, treatment in the home is generally more difficult to pursue and to monitor successfully, particularly where families are beset by a varity of other problems which do not allow them the time and space in their lives to commit themselves to such a treatment plan.

If the soiling is seen to be a form of regression in the child (secondary encopresis), then treatment will focus upon whatever stresses are seen to be producing anxiety for him. To this end, the problem of soiling can largely be ignored, since its function is primarily as an indicator of a more fundamental underlying problem. Clearly parents will need a great deal of support and encouragement if they are to ignore the encopresis, and concentrate on emotional issues within the family. If the problem does not improve, then the child may need skilled child psychotherapy in order to explore and ease his difficulties.

Where children have been under pressure because of parental fastidiousness or obsessiveness regarding toileting, then skilled social work help may help to modify their attitudes and handling of the child. This will inevitably place parents in some conflict, and work with them is likely to be challenging, and at times disagreeable. In such circumstances, the questions that parents often pose are 'Why should we modify our standards, or attitudes? Why should we tolerate such a dirty and unhygienic piece of behaviour?' They may even question the social worker's standards, if the professional response is seen to afford the sympathy and understanding to the child that they cannot themselves give. Placed in this position social workers may need frequently to remind themselves that they are not in the job just to make things easy for their clients or themselves. The ability to take on board conflicting and uncompromising parental attitudes, to evaluate and challenge these, and to sustain the relationship when 'the going gets tough', are at the heart of the social work task. This is undertaken in the sure belief that, whatever advances are made by the child in individual therapy are unlikely to be sustained, unless these are matched by some modification of attitudes in the parents.

Problems involving constipation and overflow soiling will need medical intervention in order to relieve the symptom. However, physical treatments are only likely to be successful if a trusting relationship has been established with the child. Physical treatments will only be a part of the overall treatment plan which aims to address the underlying emotional difficulties in the child. Again, parents will need some sympathy and support if they are to stay engaged in treatment. For example, where a child soils in order to express negative feelings, then improvement in the soiling may lead the child to express aggression and negativistic behaviour in other ways. Parents will need help and advice if they are to understand that their child is experimenting with more healthy ways of expressing aggressive feelings. In addition to individual social work help, parents may wish to consider joining a group of parents with similar problems, to explore common anxieties in their management of encopresis.

Where the problem has been quite long standing, then these older children will require more individual help, since parental attitudes which have been consolidated over time are likely to be quite resistant to modification.

In a follow-up study of severe encopretics (Holman, Butler & Berg, 1982) who had been treated in an in-patient unit, about 20 per cent had improved very little, whilst about half had been free of soiling for some six months. Little appears to be known about why some children appear to respond better than others.

Summary points

- Encopresis is considered abnormal after the age of 4 years, and is more common in boys than girls.
- The most common presentations of the problem are (a) primary encopresis (the child has never gained bowel control), (b) secondary encopresis (control was gained for

a period, and then lost), and (c) constipation with overflow soiling. Medical investigation will be necessary to exclude possible organic factors (e.g) Hirchsprung's Disease, anal fissure, etc.).

- The 'primary' condition is likely to respond to a programme of firm and consistent re-training, probably in a residential setting.
- The 'secondary' condition is more likely to be caused by stress or trauma in the child's life, and therapeutic intervention will need to address these underlying difficulties.
- Constipation and overflow soiling will require medical intervention initially, but within the context of a therapeutic relationship with the child.
- As with the problem of enuresis, where encopresis is a chronic problem, then specialist child psychiatric intervention may be necessary on an in-patient basis.

* * *

David, aged 8, had begun soiling at age 5, having previously achieved bowel control. The soiling had cleared up by age 6 but within six months he began to soil intermittently. At the time of referral, he was soiling daily. His parents had responded anxiously to the problem, and when this became worse, they became irritated and angry with David. He was accused of being 'lazy and dirty' in his habits, and he was often punished by them and excluded from pleasurable activities. Investigation revealed that David's soiling coincided with stressful periods in his life – at 5 he had begun school but had difficulty settling, and at 7 the family had moved from the Midlands to the North of England because of father's employment.

The parents were both in full-time work, and led extremely busy lives. Father often worked late and his wife was exhausted by the demands of her job, and the management of the three children. Weekends were, in the main, spent on visits to family in the Midlands. It seemed that neither of them had considered what impact this upheaval might have had on David, and their brisk and frenetic lifestyle left them little time or patience to talk to him about things.

Social work intervention was focused upon increasing the parents' sensitivity to David's needs by identifying and creating opportunities for more satisfying communication between parents and child. At the same time, a toileting plan was devised in which the parents would quietly remind David to visit the lavatory at regular intervals during the day. In this way his encopresis could be carefully monitored without drawing undue attention to it. Initially, the parents did not respond well to this approach, since it required a major rethinking of their roles and priorities.

After two weeks of 'therapeutic inactivity' on the parents' part, the social worker openly confronted them with their apparent lack of motivation, and reminded them of the seriousness of the problem both for David, and themselves. They expressed anger at having to rearrange their time and activities, and it became clear that the parents had not come to any agreement between themselves. The social worker offered to assist them in drawing up a schedule of the many daily activities which demanded their time and effort. The parents were then requested to agree a list of priority activities between themselves. This exercise was a test of the parents' capacity for working together on problems, and also their capacity for change.

The social worker suggested modifications in their use of time, such as foregoing some weekend visits to relatives, and replacing these with family outings, and more local visits of interest. This seemingly innocuous suggestion produced a heated reaction in mother. Her parents demanded regular visits to them in the Midlands, and she clearly feared the disapproval that their changed arrangements would invite from them. The social worker agreed to help mother in thinking how she would manage this.

Having obtained tentative agreement to this plan, the social worker offered two week's intensive intervention in order to maximise the potential for change. David's toileting was regularly monitored without the use of negative sanctions, and praise was linked to effort rather than to achievement. At the end of two weeks there was a noticeable improvement in the soiling and this provided the basis for a more long-term treatment plan. Regular sessions with the social worker ensured that difficulties in sticking to the treatment plan could be talked through, as and when they occurred.

5
Emotional Problems

Introduction

Many children that are seen, directly or indirectly, during the course of a social worker's day are likely to be suffering from some transitory emotional disturbance. We know this, not only from experience, but also from major studies of the incidence of such problems within the general population. Social workers tend to see families at their point of maximum stress, when they are striving to cope with extreme environmental and psychological pressure, such as poverty, poor housing, unemployment, illness and death. The children we encounter frequently reflect this adversity: their faces acting as a mirror for tension, conflict, and physical and mental abuse. In such circumstances the fact that a child is upset, miserable, cowed, or angry is entirely understandable. Indeed, in the face of such adversity, a cheerful smiling face might cause us to question the child's perception and assessment of the world about it.

However, on other occasions we may be confronted by children and adolescents who are displaying some form of emotional disturbance which seems unrelated to their particular environmental circumstances or inappropriate for their age. In these cases our attention may be drawn to the persistence of the particular problem, its duration and intensity, and the extent to which it interferes with normal daily life. In making such a judgement the social worker must always be aware of the danger that they might be imposing their values or beliefs about what is normal behaviour upon a

41

child or family. To this dilemma social workers must bring their knowledge and experience of normal development, a sympathetic understanding of the clients' background and culture, a knowledge of prevailing local standards and a sensitivity to the amount of distress being engendered for both parents and child.

Some very strong emotional reactions are quite normal at a certain age, but inappropriate at another. For example, anxiety about leaving home in order to go to school may be anticipated in a 5-year-old, but can generate considerable concern if observed in somebody of 14. Similarly, fears about sleeping in the dark tend to be less tolerated by parents as the child advances in years. Careful attention should always be paid to the circumstances in which behaviour is exhibited, and the tempations to leap to conclusions, without a full command of all the facts, should be avoided.

Early childhood is very frequently infused with behaviour which has an obsessional or ritualistic flavour to it. For example, rigid routines at bedtime, the avoidance of cracks in pavement, and examples of magical thinking – such as keeping some imagined disaster at bay by the performances of repetitive rituals – are quite common. But if they begin to feel to the child that they are being imposed by outside forces, and start to curtail everyday activity then they may be said to be pathological. For example, there was a boy of 14 who was unable to get dressed for school on time because he had to put on, and take off, every item of his clothing 50 times before he could leave his bedroom.

In most cases the child will gradually grow out of any difficulty, and only in rare cases do they persist into adulthood to manifest themselves as an adult neurosis. Similarly, in many instances some identifiable precipitating factor – a change of school, loss of a close friend, birth of a sibling or hospitalisation of a parent – may be identifiable.

To summarise, minor emotional problems are commonplace in childhood. If responded to sympathetically without occasioning too much reinforcement, anger or anxiety, they will subside of their own accord. However, in some cases they may persist and grow. Then the social worker may have to make the decision to call upon more expert psychological or psychiatric help. As a checklist the following points are worth bearing in mind when assessing the importance of an emotional problem:

● How persistent is it?
● How far does it extend into the child's life? Does it affect only a small area of daily activity, or is it all encompassing?
● How severe is the problem? (Are there periods when the child is better/worse?)
● Is the reaction age-appropriate?
● Are there obvious circumstances in the child's life which may account for the reaction?
● In what socio-cultural setting does the child live, and is the behaviour in harmony with that?
● Is the child able to reflect upon the problem and change in response to advice or suggestion, or does the child feel driven by a force external to itself?
● How are parents or caretakers reacting?
● Does anyone else in the family have a similar problem?

ANXIETY

A good many of the emotional and psychological problems that we discuss in this book embody varying degrees of anxiety. However, in some children anxiety, directly expressed as a feeling of fearfulness, is the main presenting problem. Anybody when presented with a threatening situation, or indeed something with which he or she is not overly familiar, is likely to exhibit signs of anxiety. Typically these include feelings of unease, palpitations, sweating, perhaps feeling sick and possibly a desire to go to the lavatory. Social workers, recalling their first home visit, should be able to conjure up the picture in their imagination! If these sensations persist, or appear in the absence of any genuine threat, then one might be said to have an anxiety state. The anxiety might be 'free-floating' or fixed upon certain objects or places in which case it is usually described as a 'phobia'. Very young children, not uncommonly. have minor phobias relating to certain types of animal and will go out of their way in order to avoid confrontation. A toddler of our acquaintance has the same reaction to the music which introduces 'Doctor Who'. In more serious cases the child will begin to suffer from broken sleep; perhaps complain of nightmares; talk of their fears of loss (usually of parents) or the worry they have about some imminent disaster.

The first task for a social worker, when encountering a child like this, is to attempt an accurate description of the anxiety and the circumstances which seem to induce it.

- Is the anxiety 'free-floating' or focused?
- If it is focused, what objects, people or places evoke it?
- Does the anxiety cause avoidance behaviour, or merely evoke feelings of distress in the individual?
- What forms does the anxiety take?
- What reaction, if any, does the anxiety provoke from other people – parents for example?
- Do panic attacks follow?
- Can the individual reduce the level of anxiety themself in any way?
- How does this symptom affect the child's normal functioning?

In many instances it may never be possible to establish definitively why somebody has developed a fear reaction, but for the purposes of intervention this is usually unnecessary. However, in some cases one of the following four contingencies may have contributed to its development:

1. The fear reaction may have developed following the experiencing or witnessing of a particular traumatic event.
2. The individual, lacking in social skills, may find that coping in certain situations is embarrassing and discomforting.
3. In some circumstances fear reactions may be acquired from other people. For example, anxious children frequently have anxious parents who do not have a very robust view of the world about them.
4. An anxious child may be reacting to what he/she perceives to be an unsettled family situation: marital disharmony;

unsettling disappearances of parent(s); worries about the health of parent(s) etc.

Management

Management of fear and anxiety, unless it is so crippling as to demand referral to a specialist agency, should normally reflect the picture which emerges from the careful assessment outlined earlier. As a general rule if the anxiety is focused then most of the effort should go upon the control of the symptoms produced. If, on the other hand, the anxiety is more generalised the emphasis should be upon environmental change and social skills training for the individual. In working with children a cloudy picture may emerge and in practice a combination of approaches is often attempted.

Within the context of a Social Service Area Team it is unlikely, in our experience, that a referral will be couched in terms of child anxiety unless it is a problem related to school (cf. Chapter 7). However, minor anxiety in childhood and adolescence is a common complication of other referrals. For example, it frequently crops up in cases where we are called upon to deal with marital disharmony or child abuse. In child abuse cases a child older than the one implicated in the non-accidental injury (NAI) case may well be affected by anxiety symptoms.

In every case a good deal of work will have to be undertaken with the child's parent or carer. This will usually involve simple explanation of the phenomena, and typically an attempt to encourage the caretaker to change their behaviour towards the affected child. They may be encouraged to show less anxiety themselves in certain circumstances; to adopt a more relaxed attitude towards the child; or to ease up upon certain demands and pressures that they may be imposing.

Direct work with the child could involve one of four different interventions.

- simple desensitisation
- *in vivo* exposure

● social skills training
● simple relaxation techniques

Although each of these techniques may sound overly complicated and difficult to implement in the context of a SSD in essence they involve the systematic application of commonsense ideas. Many parents, quite unknowingly, use similar methods in the daily handling of their children. Hudson & Macdonald (1986) give an excellent introduction to their use in social work settings. An illustration of their usefulness, in dealing with a case of an anxious child, may be found by examining the case study of David at the end of this chapter.

DEPRESSION

Depression, as one might see it in adults, is uncommon in children, particularly before puberty. However, during adolescence misery and general unhappiness, sometimes extending over many months, has been noted in as many as 1 adolescent in 5. In most cases the misery is transitory, and may usually be related, quite readily, to some setback in social relationships or other stressful life event. In more serious examples the generalised feeling of misery may be accompanied by concern about physical complaints – perhaps the worry of illness – disturbed sleep, weight loss, and a general lack of interest in the world resulting in social withdrawal. Typically school performances begins to deteriorate as the individual loses interest in work and seems unable to concentrate.

Management

Generally, given time and sympathetic support, the individual will gradually pull out of the gloom on his or her own. In very rare cases, perhaps because of severe weight loss or fears about suicidal behaviour (cf. Chapter 8) some form of inpatient help, together with medication, might be necessary. More commonly the approach will be to use counselling and psychotherapeutic techniques to help the individual and their carer(s) gently to examine the present state of affairs and reflect upon possible causes. This might conceivably involve two social workers – one working directly with the child or adolescent, the other with the parent(s) or carer.

In very young children, or those with poor conceptual and language skills, play therapy might be useful as a vehicle for communication. Using toys in this way the child may be able to act out the family dynamics, and explore their own defences and coping mechanisms.

For children in care, the frequent moves that they undergo and the general uncertainty that many face, makes them particularly vulnerable to depressive feelings. Residential and day-care staff may frequently be confronted by a withdrawn and tearful child, difficult to communicate with, hostile to advances, and wretchedly miserable about their lives. One reaction, which has to be resisted by staff, is to back off from such a situation. To sit quietly with a distressed child, patiently listening to their view of the world is a painful and necessary experience. Some focus for discussion may be helpful. In recent years the constructive use of life histories and life story books has been used to this purpose. Helping to construct a life story book may help a child to hang onto, and make some sense of, their life experiences. It will also provide a structure around which conversation may be hung. Helping a child to talk about earlier separations may enable them to gain greater purchase on the events and tease out reality from phantasy. Enabling a child to mentally organise a picture of their past is a slow, difficult, and demanding task, but one which ultimately can be very rewarding. Such children may have a very low self-esteem and be only too ready to blame themselves for the unfortunate events in their lives. In such a situation suicidal thoughts may be expressed and these need to be properly assessed, and if necessary specialist help requested (cf. Chapter 11).

HYPOCHONDRIASIS

All children complain of feeling ill, having stomach pains, etc; and sometimes we may think that the symptoms are imagined or exaggerated. Most of us, at some time, have made the most out of symptoms in order to avoid doing something that we did not want to do. However, in some children, usually because they are overly anxious or feel themselves to be under some kind of stress, the pattern of complaint becomes more regular. Presenting oneself as ill begins to have some definite purpose; for example, avoidance of school or trips to the swimming pool. This behaviour may unwittingly be encouraged by parents who are overly solicitous to their child when supposedly ill. By giving the child lots of attention and comfort, when distressed, they reinforce this pattern of behaviour. Further reinforcement may accrue if the child is taken to a variety of doctors and clinics in order to establish some physical basis for a problem which is essentially psychological.

Management

The starting point in such cases should be first to establish an accurate picture of the problem; when does it occur; how frequently; are there any precipitants; what are the advantages and benefits of hanging on to this symptom? Next, an attempt should be made to identify any stressors in the child's life: do they have worries about school; are they unhappy about changing their clothes in front of other children; are they witnessing family conflict?

The social worker may then typically work along three lines of approach. First, might come some attempt to change the circumstances of the child's life so that the stress factor is reduced or removed altogether. Secondly, some direct work may be attempted with the child to enable them to deal with the anxiety in a more appropriate way. This may involve some rehearsal of social situations, so that they learn how to cope in a different way, or perhaps social skills training. Finally, some work is usually necessary with the parents. They must be encouraged to be less protective of the child and to control their feelings when symptoms are presented. They have to learn how to deal with them in a more matter of fact way. At the same time they should be encouraged to pay more attention to the child when he or she *is not* displaying the symptoms of illness.

In some extreme cases the child may simply be so emotionally starved or neglected that becoming ill is the only way that they have to command affection. In such cases of extreme emotional impoverishment some effort may be required to provide a substitute caretaker. This may involve a fostering arrangement or more simply finding somebody who is prepared to spend time with the child or adolescent on a regular basis.

HYSTERIA

Both hysterical conditions and those that we describe in the next section (obsessional–compulsive disorders) are less likely to be encountered by an area team social worker than those illustrated earlier. Nonetheless, it is important for a social worker to be aware of the typical presentation in such cases so that, if necessary, they may be appropriately referred to another agency such as a child guidance clinic, child psychologist or child psychiatrist.

Hysterical problems may easily be confused with some form of physical disorder. Indeed in some instances the child may have undergone considerable medical examination and testing before it has been decided that the problem is psychological rather than biological in origin. Typically what is exhibited by the child or adolescent is some form of paralysis, disturbance of sensation, fit or deafness. Extremely rare in the young child, the condition becomes more common in adolescence where an imbalance of 3 to 1 in favour of females to males establishes itself. Periodically this strange disorder seems to reach almost epidemic proportions when, usually in some form of institutional setting, a wave of fainting fits or convulsions cuts a swathe through the, generally, female population. In such circumstances, at least initially, some external cause is sought as an explanation. Recently noxious fumes were blamed for an outbreak of fainting at a music festival. Upon closer investigation it became clear that no external agent was to blame. Rather, a heightened emotional climate in combination with one or two susceptible individuals seems to have been sufficient to spark off the imitative behaviour. Hyperventilation leading to giddyness and eventual faints is a commonly cited mechanism in this phenomenon.

A number of models have been advanced to explain this puzzling problem and most seem to follow some variant of psychoanalytic theory (Freud, 1977). Usually it is described as a defence mechanism which is invoked in order to deal with some form of anxiety. The ego is seen as defending itself against the anxiety by converting it into a bodily dysfunction. Overlaid on this seems to be a degree of learned behaviour. If the bodily symptom is taken seriously by family and medical staff then various secondary gains accrue. The 'patients' became subject to a good deal of attention and possibly affection which might otherwise be denied to them. They are thereby 'rewarded' for displaying the symptoms and the pathological behaviour becomes reinforced. By the time that hysteria is suspected the individuals have adjusted to their sick role and find it quite comfortable. The psychological problem may also take on a physical dimension. For example, the child with a hysterical paralysis of a limb can find that the joint involved begins to calcify. This deformation develops as a result of the limb and joint being held in a twisted position.

In order to break into this vicious circle some individual therapists and those responsible for establishing routines to be followed in residential units advocate that the symptoms, in so far as it is possible, should be ignored. The rationale for this is that it removes the reinforcers from the situation. This may be difficult to sustain in practice. One of the residential units with which we were involved instituted a policy of trying to ignore the 'fits' and subsequent paralysis of a 12-year-old girl. It was noticeable that the fits seemed to occur in increasingly inconvenient places after the policy was instituted. However, both staff and other residents quickly adjusted to the fact that in order to enter or leave the unit one had to step over a rigid body – casual visitors found it rather more difficult to accept!

Management

Transitory examples of hysteria may well come and go at home without coming to the attention of anybody outside the immediate family. However, those cases which become labelled as such are likely to be severe and fairly intractable. Usually lengthy and highly skilled help is required in order to effect any improvement. In many cases this will involve some form of psychotherapy with the child and intensive casework with the parent(s) or caretaker. However, some therapists have attempted to use family therapy methods whilst others adopt a behavioural model of treatment.

OBSESSIONAL-COMPULSIVE DISORDERS

Obsessional thoughts may be said to occur when ideas, images or words repetitively and persistently come to mind. Acting out of the obsessional thoughts, particularly when it leads to repetitive behaviour, may be described as compulsive. The individuals feel compelled, for their own comfort, to repeatedly wash their hands, or systematically touch a particular object, for example.

All of us, at some time, have experienced obsessive-compulsive behaviour, and it is particularly common in young children. For example, many children seem to develop a very strict routine around bedtimes and getting dressed which takes on a ritualistic flavour. Residential staff quickly become aware of this among the children in their charge. Similarly, many children's games have a repetitive and ritualistic pattern such as those which involve not walking on the cracks in the pavement. Intrusive thoughts such as 'if the next bus is a red one my mummy will get better in hospital', are also common in childhood, particularly if the child concerned is distressed in some way. How many social workers, on their way to a court appearance, have felt the need to check that their files are *really* in their briefcase, even though rationally they know that they cannot have jumped out?

As in many similar instances drawing the line between what

is normal and what pathological is sometimes difficult. One of the adolescents that we were working with delighted his employer when, upon leaving school, he began work in his shop. The shopkeeper was particularly pleased about the care with which he handled money, always carefully checking the change before passing it to the customer. However, the employer soon became agitated as the time taken to check the change extended to the point at which the employee could never actually bring himself to hand over the money for fear of mistake!

As a phase in normal development the behaviour is usually fairly mild, short-lived, performed without anxiety or distress, and able to be relinquished, if necessary, under mild parental pressure. In the case of a pathological presentation it is usually maintained for a longer period, and the child is likely to be ill at ease, and 'out of step' with his social environment.

The problem, if severe, frequently becomes entangled with, and affects, family relationships. Commonly another close family member will have displayed obsessional symptoms at some time and the household may be characterised by an undue emphasis upon cleanliness, order and propriety. The adolescent may draw other family members into the obsessional thoughts and compulsive behaviour or use it to exert control in a manipulative kind of way. Reactions, for parents, may well be punitive as tempers begin to fray, and this in turn can inflame guilty or ambivalent feelings that the offspring might harbour.

Management

In most cases, except for those exhibiting only the mildest of difficulty, intervention is best left to some form of specialist service. Explanations for obsessive–compulsive behaviour abound in the literature and focus mainly on either a psychoanalytic or a behavioural explanation of the disorder. However, there is general agreement that it is some form of defensive behaviour in reaction to an anxiety provoking threat. Psychoanalysts invoke notions of a pathological ego defence mechanism such as reaction formation or isolation. Behaviorists on the other hand perceive the problems as emanating from a learned avoidance response or a cognitive set in which the individual sufferers have a tendency to see events in their lives as inevitably threatening and doomed to turn out badly.

Adherents to the first school of thought would offer to sufferers a programme involving extensive talk about their life and problems – psychotherapy or psychoanalysis. The behaviorists on the other hand may opt for a programme of modelling whereby the subject is exposed to a variety of alternative ways of coping – residential staff frequently, knowingly or unknowingly, take on this role (Bandura, 1977). Other techniques, which have proved successful in adults, such as thought-stopping, may also be tried. Here the adolescent is taught how to interrupt the obsessive thoughts. He or she is encouraged to practice actually saying 'Stop', when the obsessive thoughts begin, and then deliberately attempting to focus their thoughts upon some other subject (Bellack & Hersen, 1977). In a residential setting, such as an assessment centre or childrens' home, such programmes may be quite practicable if the care staff work under the supervision of someone who is trained in this field such as a clinical psychologist.

For the field social workers much of their effort may be concentrated upon work with the parents. This may involve explanation and some attempt to get the parents to adopt a more relaxed attitude towards their child. Frequently, in such cases, by the time outside help is called upon, family and child are locked into an emotional battle which may have developed as secondary to the original symptoms. Taking the heat out of this new situation may help all concerned to see the world more clearly, and allow the child or adolescent some emotional space in which to develop and hopefully change.

*　　　*　　　*

David – a case study of anxiety

The original referral to the SSD came from a health visitor who was concerned about the danger of non-accidental injury to David's younger brother Gareth, who was nearly 3. However, in the course of work with Gareth's mother, who was a single parent, the social worker allocated to the case was also concerned about David, who had just had his tenth birthday.

David was a timid miserable child who looked undernourished and had missed a good deal of school because of apparent stomach pains and feelings of nausea. His mother was a complex woman who seemed to blow hot and cold towards him – on the one hand she could be anxious and overprotective, on the other apparently cold and rejecting. She had a history of psychiatric admissions for depressive illnesses and was currently on medication from her GP for what she described as 'my nerves'.

David was an intelligent and sensitive boy who had few friends his own age. He had a particular fear of large dogs, which he would at times cite as the reason for his reluctance to leave the house. This appeared to emanate from an event that happened when he was about 5. A large dog chased after him in the street, he slipped on making an escape and received severe gravel-rash to his knees and thighs. He also had some 'free-floating' anxiety which seemed to be related to going out of the house unaccompanied and in particular the thought of meeting other children.

The main focus of the social work task was still the infant Gareth, but the social worker thought it prudent to try to ease some of the pressure upon the mother. David's difficulties seemed to contribute to the feelings that she had about being unable to cope so became, in the view of the social worker, a legitimate target for intervention.

The social worker's analysis of David's problem was as follows: his free-floating anxiety could be attributed to his mother's ambivalence about him, her periods of absence due to hospitalisation, and the possibility that he had 'learned' some of his anxiety from her; the specific anxiety about dogs could be related to the painful events of some five years before; finally, he seemed to be lacking in certain social skills resulting in few peer contacts.

The fear of dogs was tackled, with assistance from his mother, by a programme of desensitisation. The first step was to draw up, with David, a hierarchical listing of his fears regarding dogs. At the top of this list, evoking most anxiety, was being chased by a large black dog; somewhere in the middle were ideas such as meeting a small dog under the control of its owner; at the bottom of the hierarchy, and least provocative of anxiety, was merely seeing a dog out of the window. A plan was then drawn up whereby David could gradually work his way up this hierarchy. Initially this simply involved him in sitting comfortably in a chair and then trying to conjure up, in his imagination, one of the threatening images. When he became anxious he was taught how to control this by slowly saying over to himself the phrase, 'I am in control, I must stay calm'. Very slowly the social worker encouraged him to move up the hierarchy, gradually increasing the size of the stress factor.

A near neighbour had a small white dog and he was introduced to this cautiously at first until he could bring himself to touch it. The neighbour, who was elderly, also happened to be one of the social worker's clients. She was beginning to find that taking the dog for a walk was becoming too much for her to manage every day. David eventually agreed that he would undertake this for her. Regularly exercising the dog seemed to be sufficient to enable David to overcome his other dog related fears. It also seemed to increase his social confidence and he found going out of the house easier to manage with a dog on a lead. He also seemed to acquire some kudos from some of the other local children. However, he still seemed to be experiencing some difficulty in relating to his peers so the final part of the plan involved introducing him to a small IT group which was being started by a specialist worker in the area team. Part of the focus for this group was social skills training.

A few months later David was able to join the local scout group, and was even prepared to consider a weekend away with them camping.

Unfortunately, his mother's mental health began to deteriorate and her eventual hospitalisation led to David's departure to foster parents, this time for a protracted stay.

Initially Gareth accompanied his mother to hospital, but eventually he joined his brother in the foster home.

*   *   *

Gail - a case study of depression

Gail was twelve when she arrived at the family group home. She had been in and out of Care since the age of four. Her single-parent mother had been neglectful over the years, and at one time abuse had been suspected. In all she had spent five periods in care for spells of up to six months at a time either with foster-parents or in a large children's home. Her mother, who had been hospitalised intermittently throughout this time, always insisted upon her returning home when she managed to establish herself again.

The transfer to the group home followed an admission to Care for yet another period in hospital for her mother and the subsequent breakdown of a fostering arrangement. Some three weeks after joining the group home it was learned that Gail's mother had died in hospital of stomach cancer.

Initially Gail seemed unconcerned about the bereavement. Normally a lively, extroverted girl she continued to attend the local school and appeared matter of fact about the trauma. The staff, perhaps under the impression that she was coping with the loss in a grown-up way, tended to steer clear of mentioning her mother's death. Some three months later Gail was felt by the staff to be becoming 'difficult to handle'. She seemed unusually resistant to the normal rules and routines of the home, irritable in the mornings and meal times, and spiteful to the other residents. Gradually they noted that she was spending more time on her own and that, complaining of headaches and vague back pains, she was taking odd days off school. Her decline rapidly progressed as she started to lose weight, appeared to be lost in her own thoughts for much of the time and liable to burst into tears at the smallest comment or criticism about her.

Following a case conferences it was decided that Gail's key worker should, with the support of a senior social worker, begin to set aside a regular hour every three days to spend with Gail in order to talk about her difficulties.

Initially Gail resisted, sometimes quite angrily, any attempt to encourage her to talk about her past. However gradually, as more trust developed, the session would be filled with Gail's uncontrollable, and unprovoked, sobbing. After three weeks of this, during which time the key worker, feeling helpless, wanted to pull out of the contract, things began to improve. Gail was still very miserable and uneasy, but she agreed that an effort ought to be made in order to think about the times that she had spent with her mother when alive. At the worker's prompting it was agreed that some attempt be made to reconstruct and chart their life together. Slowly a scrapbook was built up timetabling Gails's life. It was illustrated with old christmas cards, a few photos of her mother and some new photographs taken of the various places in which she had lived over the past twelve years. This last activity involved some short car trips with the social worker and Gail becoming interested in and adept at taking her own photographs.

The misery about the loss of her mother now became tinged, at times, with strong expressions of anger: 'How could she leave me?'; 'She never wanted me, I hate her'. Some of this verbal barrage the key worker also found painful to sit through, but with regular supervision she was encouraged to stick with it. After a further three months Gail's mood had markedly changed. She gradually became less tearful and verbally aggressive and for the first time evidenced some interest in future plans – a proposed school trip during the Easter holiday.

After a further six months she left the home in order to join some foster parents who had gradually been introduced to her.

6
Anti-Social or Conduct Problems

Introduction

There can be few areas of work with which the social worker is involved about which so much conflicting evidence has been generated and so many words written as anti-social behaviour. For example, the subject of delinquency has exercised countless minds, and produced libraries of books – few of which reach any compelling conclusions. We have chosen in this chapter to present no more than a sketch of this territory. We have been mindful of the need to indicate areas of further reading and of the fact that a number of the other texts in this series cover this area more deeply. For example, books in the Practical Social Work series such as *Working with Offenders* (Walker & Beaumont, 1985) and *Youth Work* (Jeffs & Smith, 1987) all make a contribution.

Definitions

As soon as one begins to examine some of the definitions and terms used in this field the cause of so much debate and contention becomes apparent. These difficulties become compounded when the focus shifts to notions of causation and management. Conduct disorders are usually considered to be those in which the main problem lies in socially disapproved behaviour. But to whom is the behaviour unacceptable and what currency do their standards have? If the socially-disapproved-of behaviour also happens to be against the Law

57

then it is called juvenile delinquency. If, in turn, the behaviour involved the wanton damage or destruction of property then the term 'vandalism' is invoked. Typically the type of behaviours covered by this rubric include: aggressive behaviour; bullying; persistent lying; stealing; truanting; destructiveness and defiance etc. The definitional problems should not need too much spelling out. Much of this behaviour is universal in children and young people. For example, the majority of children (63 per cent) have stolen something significant at school at some time. The crucial factors may then become: who objects to the behaviour? Who has the power to label it? how persistent is the behaviour and in what context does it occur? In many cases the 'disorder' may have as much to do with societal reaction as it has to the behaviour of the individual.

Prevalence

If definitions are rather loose and contentious it follows that estimating prevalence is bedevilled with problems. The best attempt to arrive at an estimate of conduct disorders was that made by Rutter and his colleagues. In two major surveys they examined the population of 10–11-year-olds on the Isle of Wight (Rutter *et al.*, 1970) and a sample of children in an Inner London Borough (Rutter *et al.*, 1975). Their findings seemed to confirm two widely-held beliefs. First, that conduct disorders are far more common in boys than girls. Second, that the prevalence tends to be higher in inner city areas than in rural areas. The figures that emerged from this extensive screening of the general population were that about 2 per cent of the Isle of Wight population, and 4 per cent of those in Inner London displayed signs of conduct disorder. One other finding which emerged subsequently and which is of significance to both social workers and teachers was the strong association between conduct disorders and reading difficulties.

Models of understanding

A large number of theoretical models, which attempt to explain conduct disorder and delinquency, have been constructed over the years. Many reflect wider beliefs, current at the time, about human behaviour. Some of these models contradict each other and are built upon fairly sparse evidence. Advocates of a particular point of view easily become embroiled in interminable and rather arid debate with those who take up a contrary position. At various times people have held that conduct disorders and delinquent acts are explicable in terms of a genetic abnormality; a disturbance of the brain; and, a deficit in the autonomic nervous system. Most of this bio-medical evidence is disputed by sociologists and psychologists who prefer to see the problem, as resulting from faulty social learning; inadequate life opportunities and social injustice; deficits in social skills; peer group pressure; or faulty family interactions.

The debate is further complicated when one focuses upon 'official' delinquency. This adds another dimension since factors such as detection and action by the police have to be taken into account. Many contend that this process reflects societal attitudes towards certain groups in our society such as blacks, adolescents from poorer homes, or those who live in certain sectors of our inner cities. They, it is argued, are picked out and labelled as deviant for behaviour which if seen in other sectors of the population would be overlooked or handled in some other way.

At this level of theorising it may appear that there is little of practical value to the busy social worker. We have some sympathy with the rather jaundiced views of Morgan (1979). She contends that there is little evidence to support any of the various explanatory theories that are advanced. They are put forward, and clung to, she believes because professional feel 'comfortable' grasping on to a theory rather than facing up to the fact that they do not really have an adequate explanation for something. Treating theory as if it were fact gives us a false reassurance, and, an unrealistic belief that something can be done in order to counter delinquent behaviours.

At a rather less elevated level of theorising attempts have been made to examine the backgrounds from which delinquents emerge. This does at least begin to offer the possibility of some form of social work intervention.

For example, West & Farrington (1973) compared the families of delinquents and non-delinquents and felt that the following differences emerged. Delinquents were, in their view, more like to come from:

   (i) a low income family;
  (ii) a large family;
 (iii) a family the parents of which were of low intelligence;
 (iv) a family, the parents of which had a criminal record;
  (v) a family that displayed 'poor parental behaviour'.

This last point is explored more fully by Patterson and co-workers in the United States (Patterson, 1982). They attempted to describe the style and pattern of parenting found most frequently in the delinquent's family. They concluded that the following characteristics were typical:

    (i) greater use made of physical punishment;
   (ii) inconsistency in the interactions between parents and children;
  (iii) few shared pleasurable activities;
  (iv) apparent lack of affection for the children;
   (v) failure to acknowledge and/or reinforce appropriate behaviour;
  (vi) poor supervision of the child;
 (vii) the rules of appropriate conduct were rarely laid down;
(viii) an inability to give clear messages about the rightness or wrongness of a behaviour.

Information such as this, which finds echoes in many other studies, does present us with the possibility of beginning to frame successful interventions. Conduct disorders and delinquency are clearly complex, multi-factorial problems. In many instances as the child matures and learns different styles of behaviour the difficulties decrease and disappear spontaneously. However, in those clients where the problems persist the most helpful interventions would appear to be those which seek to involve the parent(s) or carers and the child in a joint attempt to examine the difficulties and search for appropriate solutions.

Management

Many would agree with Sula Wolff (1977), the child psychiatrist, that 'There is no evidence for the successful treatment of antisocial children with psychotherapeutic or social casework techniques, although this does not mean that such methods are not effective for some patients.' Direct work, on a one-to-one basis, with youngsters has a long tradition and usually involves an attempt to unravel the antecedents, content and consequences of their behaviour. However, good evidence as to the effectiveness of all this effort is rather thin on the ground.

The best way forward would appear to be to pursue models of management which lay stress upon the interactional nature of the problems. These models emphasise the need to involve parent(s) or carer(s) in the change process. This requires, as we have stressed elsewhere in this book, that a start be made by making a careful analysis of the present situation. Many of the techniques that we will go on to describe are equally applicable to both the home and the residential setting. In the latter, care staff simply take the role assigned to parents.

Usually conduct-disordered children arrive at the doors of an area social service office because of some complaint(s) on the part of the parent(s). In the case of children in residential care it is usually staff or other children who are the complaintants. Only rarely do the young persons bring themselves to the attention of a social worker. This is rather different from, say, a child with an anxiety state who may seek out help and therefore co-operate with those who offer it. The initial problem for the social worker may then be that the young person does not perceive their behaviour as problematic; may find it quite pleasurable; and, may not have the least desire to change. In some cases of delinquency, when the police are involved, the individual's anger and resentment may also pose an insurmountable barrier to an effective intervention.

Typically the complaint is a very general one: 'I can't do a thing with him', 'She doesn't listen to a word I say, she just runs wild and does what *she* wants'. If the parent is concerned enough to approach a social worker for help this may be indication enough that the problem is of long standing and that the parent is very worked up about it. However, it is always worth examining the possibility that the parent has unrealistic expectations of the child, and that the real problem is their ideas about appropriate standards of behaviour. The next task is simply to listen and allow the parent to let off steam. From this begins to emerge a picture of the way in which the parent perceives the problem. The complaints are usually rather vague and over generalised. To say that somebody is 'out of control', or 'running wild' conveys very little. For example, it would be very unusual for somebody to be 'out of control' all the time. It becomes important to establish some or all of the following points:

● when is the person *in* control
● what seems to lead up to them losing control?
● is the loss of control related to certain events, sequences of events, times of day or certain people?
● what *actually* happens during these periods of no control?
● what, if anything or anybody, is able to help in reasserting control?

An angry or distraught parent will present a global picture and will need time in order to describe and accurately locate the problems that they are having. This process, by enabling them to see the problem more clearly, may alter their perspective and give them renewed confidence in dealing with it. In our experience many parents find that having talked over their difficulties with regard to a particular child, they are able to return home with new confidence in their own parenting skills. As well as an overly generalised picture, parents may also be unclear about which of their children is actually causing them most difficulty. In some cases an 'innocent' child attracts all the blame for the others. Calmly listing the problems and trying accurately to locate the difficulties is the first step to understanding.

Once this process of clarification has been completed some direct work, particularly with older children, may prove helpful. However, it is our belief that parents or carers are usually the keys to an effective intervention for the following reasons:

- the parents' (carers') own behaviour may cause or maintain the conduct disorder;
- parents are rightfully the people who should exercise any necessary control over their children;
- because the parents usually see far more of their children than anybody else they are the people best placed to effect behavioural change;
- the problem may be related to difficulties with either brothers or sisters: here too, parents are best placed to appreciate this and ultimately act upon it.

Good parenting is usually regarded as involving a combination of the following factors: consistency; even-handedness towards all the children; adequate affection; and opportunities for growth and learning. In many instances the child's problems may be located in the inadequate or ineffective performance of these task by the parents. However, by the time that the problem reaches a social worker it is usually too late to restore the situation simply by seeking to establish patterns of good parenting. Before that may be done some form of intervention is usually required in order to recreate some familial stability and harmony. In attempting to do this our own practice has been heavily influenced by the work of the McAuleys (McAuley & McAuley, 1977, 1980, 1982), who are advocates of parent training. For a fuller review of their work readers are advised to examine the excellent text by Hudson & Macdonald (1986).

The McAuleys typically use three types of interventions in their work: time-outs; differential attention; and a points system. The first two appear to be most helpful with children under about 7, the third is more effective with children aged between 7 and 12.

Time-outs

Time-outs are a response to undesired behaviour. The objective is to give children little or no social reinforcement for their actions. This does not mean necessarily that the child is sent from the room – say to his or her own bedroom. This may not be very helpful, particularly if that room contains toys and books. The opportunity to play thus provided may be perceived as a reinforcement for the undesired behaviour and thereby encourage its continuation.

The MaAuleys (1977) recommend that three stages be delineated. Progress from one stage to the next being determined by the failure to comply:

(1) clear commands by the parent;
(2) command repeated with the 'time-out' threat;
(3) use of 'time-out'.

Hobbs & Forehand (1977) in reviewing the effectiveness of this technique suggest the following eight steps:

(1) give clear reasons to the child for adopting the procedure;
(2) keep a record of the times that it is used;
(3) consider whether to remove the child or the source of social reinforcement (e.g. mother or sibling);
(4) issue a single warning before implementation;
(5) ensure that the place to which the child is sent is not rewarding. This may be the corner of the room, or another room which offers little opportunity for stimulation. This does not mean locking them in the coal-cellar!
(6) use the procedure on every occasion at the beginning;
(7) the duration should be no more than five minutes – less if compliance is good;
(8) gradually fade out the procedure. Do not reduce the duration of the time out, but use it intermittently.

Differential attention

This is basically an operant technique which may be taught to parents or carers. It involves quite simply ignoring undesirable behaviours but paying attention to (reinforcing) desirable ones. Social workers, in our experience, often quite unconsciously use a similar technique in their everyday interviewing. Attention is paid to certain aspects of the conversation, and 'rewarded' by such cues as head-noddings, smiling, etc. However, other parts of the conversation, which are considered to be either less realistic or useful to the client, may be treated more coolly. Parents may need to rehearse some of the positive cues and be encouraged to offer praise or other verbal rewards to their children.

Points-systems

Non-compliance, particularly among adolescents, is very common. In younger children very simple rewards may be sufficient to encourage and reinforce desired behaviour. For example, we describe elsewhere the star-chart system for bed-wetting. In older children this may not be sufficient and parents begin to assume that rewards must always be seen in terms of money. Even with older children this is not always necessary and a cumulative points system which results in a 'treat' such as a day out or a trip to a football match or cinema may be effective.

When considering a scheme the following six points are worth bearing in mind:

(1) make sure that very clear demands are made of the child. They know, in other words, exactly what behaviour is required of them in order to acquire a point. It is often useful to ask the child to repeat the instruction so that you or the parent can be assured that they understand them;
(2) a fixed schedule of rewards or points should be established – no negotiation is permissible around this once the programme has begun;
(3) specify the times at which the points may be exchanged for rewards;
(4) avoid very large rewards – these usually take too long to acquire;
(5) the behaviour is what earns the point or reward not the attitude of the child or the way that something is done. Compliance is the objective;

(6) establish at the beginning of the programme if and how points may be deducted.

As the child matures, these techniques become less applicable and the adolescent increasingly expects that his or her point of view must be heard and taken account of. The role for the social worker now becomes that of mediator between parent(s) and child. Interactions between the two parties frequently become overheated, unrealistic and distorted by the strong emotion which may be generated.

The role of mediator may involve teaching the parties involved some negotiating skills (Kifer *et al.*, 1974). The objective is to encourage parents and child to examine their own positions, develop some give and take and facilitate a mutually acceptable outcome. Typically the following skills need to be cultivated:

(1) the ability to see things from another's point of view;
(2) an ability to define clearly what the problems are;
(3) a willingness to generate and consider a range of solutions;
(4) an ability to look at proposed solutions in terms of possible outcomes;
(5) skill in choosing solutions which maximise the benefits to all the parties;
(6) an ability to implement the agreed solutions.

The social worker, in order to facilitate the development of these skills, may adopt a number of techniques:

(1) encouraging ventilation of thoughts and feelings;
(2) asking the parties to write down and order both problems and solutions;
(3) role-play exercises, where people are encouraged to act out different situations and attempts at problem-solving;
(4) use of the self as a role-model;
(5) brain-storming sessions to develop innovative solutions;
(6) self-reflection;
(7) role-reversal exercises in order to encourage an individual to see another person's point of view.

Outcome

Many conduct disorders clear up spontaneously. A stable family or carer able to withstand the pressure generated by the young person and respond sympathetically and consistently is a good indicator of a favourable outcome. The child's own personality, patterns of friendship and educational or other opportunities for growth are also important.

Failure to resolve the problems appears to have an important carry-over into adult life. Severe and intractable conduct disorders in childhood and adolescence may be a precursor to adult psychiatric illness, continued anti-social behaviour, subsequent brushes with the law, and an unstable marriage (Robins, 1966; Rutter, 1980).

Prevention

In the absence of very much clear-cut evidence about the effectiveness of intervention the focus, not unreasonably, has turned towards the idea of prevention. The prevention of conduct disorders, or even delinquency, is an attractive idea but one fraught with almost as many problems as intervention. At best one may advance tentative suggestions based upon the best available evidence. Even then few of the interested parties are likely to agree upon the agenda or the ordering of priorities.

Philip Graham (1977) considered that three broad areas should be addressed: the familial, the institutional and the socio-environmental. Many of the ideas which go to make up these broad categories have profound implications for social work. More so, as the development of patch-based models of social service delivery herald a move away from a crisis-based approach towards one which espouses community development.

Using Graham's tripartite division some of the following issues bear close consideration.

The familial

(1) Parent skills training. This might begin at school.
(2) The development of family-centres.

(3) Family planning advice, abortion counselling, etc.
(4) Attempts to discourage early marriages.
(5) Early adoption of children whose biological parents cannot look after them adequately.
(6) Improvements to child-care services. Wide use of fostering arrangemens, etc.
(7) Greater availability of marital counselling services.
(8) Improved financial supports to single-parent families.

Institutional

(1) Increased nursery and pre-school education.
(2) Improvements within schools:
   smaller classes
   more help for slow learners
   school counsellors
   special schemes for poor readers
(3) Improvements to hospital regimes:
   avoidance of unnecessary admissions;
   more mother and child units;
   improvements to play and visiting facilities.

Socio-environmental

(1) Improvements in housing and in particular the demise of tower-blocks.
(2) Better play-facilities particularly in the inner city.
(3) Lowered rates of unemployment and improved prospects for school-leavers.
(4) Attempts to improve road safety and lower lead levels particularly in the inner city.
(5) Increased youth club and sporting facilities.

Summary points

● Anti-social or conduct problems commonly occur in children and adolescents.
● Most will resolve themself as the individual matures.

- Widespread debate rages around both the definition and cause of such problems.
- Inadequate parenting would appear to be a major contributory factor in some cases.
- Interventions should, where possible, involve parents or carers.
- A number of behavioural techniques such as time-outs, differential attention and a points reward system may be helpful.
- A number of preventive strategies suggest themselves; some of these fall within the ambit of a SSD.

*   *   *

Time-out – a case study

Karen, who is 8, persistently irritates and teases her younger sister. This is a particular problem when they are both watching television and increasingly results in violent fights. Karen's parents are told to say very firmly and clearly when this happens – 'Karen, stop upsetting your sister'. When she persists in this her parents then say, 'Karen, stop upsetting your sister or you will have to stand in the corner'. Finally, Karen is told very firmly, but quite calmly, to stand in the corner not facing the television for two minutes. Nobody talks to her, or refers to her, during this period. At the end of the two minutes she is calmly told that she can return to the family circle in front of the television.

*   *   *

Case study

John, who is 11, has lived in a children's home for some two years. The care staff complained that since changing school he had become reluctant to get up, slow to dress and a nuisance in the bathroom every morning.

A simple programme was drawn up with the staff and John in order to remedy this. It was made very clear what was expected of him each morning and what the time limit was for him to arrive washed and dressed for breakfast. For every morning that he met the target he was to be awarded one point. With the accumulation of five points he was to be allowed to go ice-skating, of which he was very fond. After the first week only two points had been earned. No trip was forthcoming and the plan was rehearsed with him once again. Within four more weeks his performance had improved to the extent that ice-skating was becoming a regular weekly event.

7

School Attendance Problems

Introduction

The problem of non-attendance at school has existed for as long as schooling. The introduction of the Elementary Education Acts of 1870 and 1876, which made school free and compulsory, added a legal dimension to what was already regarded as an educational and social problem. Under the 1944 Education Act parents are required by Section 36 to ensure that their children receive education 'suitable to their age, ability and aptitude'. Moreover, under Section 39 they also have to ensure regular attendance. The local authority education department is empowered under Section 40 to prosecute parents if they fail in this duty. The child concerned may also be brought before the magistrates in the Juvenile Court under Section 1 of the 1969 Children and Young Persons Act for the consideration of 'care proceedings' if in the view of the bench the child is in need of 'care and control'.

In order to 'police' the legislation that developed to enforce school attendance, school board officers were appointed. They were charged with investigating and acting upon cases of poor school attendance. The 'board man' became a significant figure in the popular mythology of childhood. Many a reluctant school attender has been threatened by a desperate parent that the 'board man will come and take you away if you don't get off to school'. In recent years the education welfare officer (EWO), as he became known, has been encouraged to adopt a rather wider brief. *The Ralphs Report*, which appeared in 1972, recommended that EWOs should receive social work training. In order to reflect this

71

shift in emphasis some LEAs changed the title of this branch of their work to the 'Educational Social Work Service'. Departments began to offer an advisory service to schools, and to provide counselling to both school absentees and their families. However, the picture across the country is very varied: trained staff have been difficult to recruit and retain, and the image of the 'school bobby' still permeates many departments' work.

The figures for school attendance have shown a remarkable stability both over time and from area to area. Most surveys have indicated that on any day about 90 per cent of children will be in school. However, when it comes to the explanation of non-school attendance no such consensus exists.

At least three interlocking, and to some extent competing, views of non-school attendance are current. The first, typically held by many child psychiatrists and psychologists, locates the problem within the child or his or her family. Non-school attendance is regarded by them as a symptom of some emotional or psychological disturbance in the child or the family. Treatment in such cases may focus upon these interpersonal issues, and the return to school will be seen only as a secondary goal. Second, it is possible to discern what might be described as a 'sociological' view. The focus here is upon the individual and their response or reaction to various competing societal pressures. It may be that the child feels alienated from school because of its emphasis upon formal competitive academic work. On the other hand, the child's behaviour may reflect a sub-culture in which education – particularly at a time of high unemployment – may be regarded as irrelevant. Finally, there are those who look to the characteristics of the school and or the teachers for an explanation. They cite the size of school; the constant shifting of classrooms; the attitude of the teacher to the child, style of discipline; and emphasis upon attainment as factors. They point to the fact that the school is supposed to provide an environment which fosters both academic *and* social development.

Each of these various explanations tend to be advanced by particular professional interest groups and reflect a partial view of what is usually a multifactorial problem requiring careful behavioural analysis and close team-work for its resolution. In summary, then, a variety of explanations exist:

- a symptom of disturbance, psychiatric or psychological, in the child;
- pathological family dynamics;
- the child's (realistic?) view of the school as – unstimulating, irrelevant, etc.;
- a neglectful or indifferent attitude by the parents;
- a reflection of school organisation or teacher behaviour.

In the light of this conceptual confusion it is hardly surprising that a variety of different treatments and interventions are advocated and attempted. A good deal of effort has also been applied to the development of a typology of non-attendance, the assumption being that various different categories of non-attendance exist reflecting different underlying causes and ultimately requiring different responses.

Most observers, apart from that small minority who advocate the dropping of compulsory attendance, are agreed that failure to attend does represent a variety of problems and challanges. Among these are:

- the non-attender becomes educationally retarded;
- the child, whilst out of school, is at a great risk of comitting conduct disords and offending;
- non-attendance undermines discipline and order in the school;
- non-attendance is a precursor of more serious psychological problems which may continue into adulthood;
- 'policing' the system is time-consuming and expensive;
- chronic cases risk ending up in local authority care.

The incidence of non-attendance

As we have indicated at any one time about 10 per cent of school pupils are absent, though many of these will have legitimate reasons for their absence – illness, family holidays or religious observance. Trying to determine how many of this number are absent without authority is beset with definitional problems. The figure most widely accepted was generated by a DES survey conducted in 1974 which took a 'snap-shot' of all secondary and middle schools in England and Wales. On the appointed day 9.9 per cent of pupils were absent of whom 22.7 per cent were deemed to be so for no good reason, or 2.2 per cent of the schools' total. What is clear from the survey evidence is that unauthorised absence tends to rise with age, reaching a peak in the year the pupil intends to leave school, and that urban areas have a slightly higher incidence than rural ones.

Self-report surveys, such as the one conducted by Rob Mawby (1977), indicate that unauthorised absence is quite common, but in most cases only intermittent. He found, on asking a sample of 11–15-year-olds in Sheffield, that 46 per cent of boys and 50 per cent of girls admitted to having stayed away from school, without good reason, at least once in the previous twelve months. This also illustrates the fact that average figures do not really reveal the extent of serious problematic non-attendance. The daily figures may be made up of a small core of regular non-attenders, or of a floating population of occasional absentees. It is only the former group, however, which tends to come to the notice of SSDs and other agencies.

Definitions

A good deal of discussion has taken place in the literature in an attempt to define and characterise the apparent different types of unauthorised non-attendance. Hersov (1977) outlines three broad categories, which have received widespread support:

1. truants;
2. school refusers or school phobics;
3. children withheld from school by parents.

Attempts to classify problems in this way have laudable aims. The hope is that by making a differential diagnosis based upon regularly occuring constellations of background factors, consistent methods of effective treatment and or management may be developed. However, some people (Galloway, 1985) are unhappy about the way in which an essentially medical model is applied to what is in the view primarily a social or bureacratic problem. The danger, as they see it, is that problems become reified and undue emphasis is placed upon attempts to uncover some pathology in the child and or the family to the relative neglect of other rather broader social factors, such as the organisation of the school, or the 'climate' in the classroom.

Whilst accepting these reservations, and acknowledging that school non-attendance is a complex multi-factorial issue with no neat boundaries between what are essentially unique problems in each case, there does seem to be some value in accepting that Hersov's typology has proved helpful in focusing interventions, and improving outcomes.

Truants

Truants are children absent from school without either their parents knowledge or their permission. Typically they will set off to go to school but then slip away, either alone or with others, in order to roam the streets or perhaps shelter in a friend's house. They display none of the emotional distress evident in school refusers and parents are only made aware of what is going on by a letter from school or a visit from the EWO.

The truant has been described as 'a depressing picture of multiple adversities' (Farrington, 1980). Survey evidence does point to a depressing set of circumstances which accompany truancy, all too familiar to social workers. The constellation of factors include:

- a relationship with social class: the lower the social class of parent the higher the incidence of truancy;
- poor housing is related to truancy;
- parents typically show little interest in the child's progress;
- children from large families are more likely to truant;
- parental unemployment, or an erratic work record, is related to truancy;

- couples who display marital conflict are more likely to have children who truant;
- poor parenting and inconsistent disciplining of children is related to truancy;
- truants tend to be of lower intelligence and to have poor school attainment;
- truancy is related to delinquent behaviour such as stealing.

This negative view of the truant and the apparent pathology of their familial background has been challenged on two fronts. There are those, for example, who argue from a 'labelling' or social interactionist stance. They suggest that many children stay away from school at various times, but it is only those from deprived backgrounds or unresponsive parents who become labelled as truants and are pursued through the courts.

Other authors, again from a sociological view point, have criticised what they would see as the 'individualising' of the problematic behaviour. They argue that it must be seen within the context of the prevailing sub-culture and that in part non-attendance may be institutionally caused. Some support for this comes from the fact that non-attendance does rise steeply as the end of school life approaches, and from the fact that some schools appear to have higher truancy rates than others. Both findings are suggestive of a school or community influence at work.

One final group of truants should be mentioned, who may well go undetected. They are children who arrive at school, receive an attendance mark, and then disappear. This is a particular problem in large comprehensive schools where the lack of tangible boundary around the school and the constant changing of classrooms due to the streaming system and the various options available to pupils means that it is relatively easy to slip away.

Alan Butler conducted research on non-attendance in several such large comprehensives only to discover that many of the staff were baffled as to who should be in which group, and that the only way to ascertain true numbers was to conduct a snap roll-call!

School refusal or school phobia

Many of those who deal with non-school attenders accept that there is a sharp distinction between the so-called truant and the school refuser or school phobic. Berg (1969) suggests that there are four characteristics which go to make up the picture of the school refuser:

- Severe difficulty in attending school often amounting to prolonged absence;
- Severe emotional upset shown by such symptoms as excessive fearfulness, undue tempers, misery or complaints of feeling ill without obvious organic cause on being faced with the prospect of going to school;
- Staying at home when they should be at school with the knowledge of the parents at some stage in the course of the disorder;
- Absence of significant antisocial disorder such as stealing, lying, wandering, destructiveness, or sexual misbehaviour.

The term school phobia used to be applied to this state as it was assumed that the root of the problem was the young person's extreme anxiety and fear about actually entering the school. Such people do exist, but these days it is usually considered that the individual has a difficulty in leaving home or separating from parents, hence the more widely accepted term 'school refusal'. Typically such children are overprotected by their mothers and other siblings, and display few educational problems. More of the mothers are subject to affective (depression, anxiety, etc.) disorders than the general population and about one-third of the school-refusers continue to show neurotic symptoms and difficulties of adjustment well beyond the school leaving age.

Parental withholding

Parents may keep their children at home for a variety of reasons. It may be that they perceive little value in schooling and consider it a waste of time. Typically in such cases, they were poor achievers and attenders at school themselves. More commonly there are practical reasons for the child's withdrawal. The child concerned may be needed at home in some capacity either to help with family employment (milk-rounds or a market garden, for example) or to assist with caring for some of the younger children. Elder daughters are particularly susceptible to this pressure if for some reason – ill health, the need to work long hours – the mother has to be absent from the household during the day. Parental illness is not infrequently a complicating factor. The sick parent may take comfort in having the child at home, need him or her to fulfill various household tasks, or simply lack the energy to pack the child off to school regularly every day.

Material deprivation is also a factor. The child may lack some of the essential clothing for school – shoes, for example – or the basic equipment necessary to take part in various school-based activities. Various estimates suggest that this category of non-attendance accounts for the largest propor-tion of unauthorised absence, figures of around 50 per cent being quoted.

Management

Many differing forms of intervention have been attempted over the years with the non-school attender. In part these reflect the variety of causal factors implicated in this problem. But they also echo the shifting fashions in individual therapy and the changes in balance between those who emphasise the need to change the individual and those who advocate reforms in the school. Most people involved in helping non-school attenders, regardless of their orientation, are agreed upon the importance of certain key factors to this endeavour.

● Whatever the planned intervention it should be preceded by a careful noting of sound objective data about the nature of the non-attendance.
● All the parties concerned should be consulted and, where possible, involved in the planning of the intervention. In some cases this may involve a lengthy list of people – the

child; his or her parents(s); key staff at the school; the EWOs; the police; educational psychologists.

- Throughout an attempted intervention, all parties should be informed about what is going on and high level of cooperation sought from each of them.
- Re-entry to school should be attempted as soon as possible. The longer this is delayed the more entrenched the problem becomes, and the greater the risk of developing secondary problems. In the case of the truant this may involve minor delinquency or some other form of conduct disorder such as glue-sniffing. For the school refuser attachment to home, and anxiety about separation, is likely to increase.

Most observers have noted that a successful return to school is more likely if one or more of the following three criteria are fulfilled: first, that the request for help has been prompt rather than delayed; second, that the child concerned is pre-adolescent; finally, the 'child's' family is not faced with too many other social problems.

Truants

Truants are usually not attending school without their parents' knowledge. In many cases they may be having learning difficulties and slipping behind their peers in terms of school progress. Whilst away from school they run the risk of becoming involved in acts of minor delinquency and so may run up against the law in a variety of ways.

As with all forms of non-attendance an accurate picture needs to be established of the individual case.

- How long has the non-attendance been going on?
- Does it follow any particular pattern?
- Is it with or without parents' knowledge?
- Is it a solo activity or done with others?
- Is other anti-social behaviour involved?
- Does the young person receive any satisfactions from going to school?
- Do they have poor school performance?

● What is the parents' attitude: concerned, disinterested, punitive?
● Does the family suffer from other social problems?
● What other agencies are involved?
● What efforts have been made in the past to return the individual to school?

The answers one receives to questions such as these should shape the nature of the response.

If the family is confronted by other social problems, some attempt should be made at resolving them. At the same time very direct and strenuous efforts should be made to get the young person back to school as soon as possible. This may involve a mixture of counselling; cajoling; explanation of the legal consequences to both parents and taking the individual directly to school.

Problems within the school should also be examined. For example: is the non-attender subject to bullying? is he struggling academically in a particular class? might a change of stream be beneficial? does he require specialist teaching of some kind?

This form of brisk and direct intervention may be sufficient to break the patterns of non-attendance and encourage a speedy return. If this is successful very close monitoring of the situation should be maintained so that any future absences are responded to immediately.

In more entrenched cases the threat, or reality, of legal action may be an effective agent for change. However, this may need to be supplemented by a behavioural programme which relies upon the creation of contingency contracts. This will involve the social worker in discussing the situation with pupil, parent and school in order to undertake a functional analysis of the situation, and the events which seem to support and maintain it. Next, a contract will have to be negotiated with the parties concerned which seeks to establish an attainable set of objectives and an appropriate set of rewards or incentives for the young person.

School refusal

School refusal, or school phobia usually presents either as anxiety about leaving the home, or as anxiety about entry into school. This may be accompanied by complaints about physical symptoms, for example headaches or stomach pains, and in rarer instances actual vomiting.

Because the problem is essentially one of separation and anxiety it has to be handled rather differently from truancy. Again, one begins by a very careful analysis of the situation, and it is upon the basis of this information that one attempts to move forward.

In certain cases it may be sufficient to counsel the parent(s) about how they handle the situation in the morning and try to help them to respond rather differently. Parents quickly become involved with their child's anxiety and may consciously or unconsciously reinforce it or even on occasions encourage it. Helping the parents to examine the part they play in the problem may be a suitable starting point.

In more severe cases it may be necessary to begin a programme of systematic densitisation. This simply means that in an organised and progressive way the child is gradually exposed to and encouraged to confront and come to terms with the situations that they find anxiety–provoking. This may be done either by helping the child to relax and then getting them to run over the anxiety-provoking situations in their minds, or actually taking them gently through a graded set of experiences so that they gradually learn to feel comfortable with and in control of previously anxiety-provoking situations or settings.

The use of the court

As we described earlier, there are two routes which may be followed with regard to legal action and non-school attendance. Under the terms of the 1944 Act parents may be taken to the magistrate's court, and face an escalating level of fines, if by virtue of their apathy, wilfulness, or inability they are unable to maintain their child's regular attendance at school. The other route which may be adopted utilises the 1969 Children and Young Persons Act. Here the Juvenile Bench, being mindful of the 'best interests of the child', may consider that non-attendance is symptomatic of the need for care, protection or control. In such cases the court may opt to take the child into Care or more usually assign to it a supervision order under the authority of a social worker. However, the terms of the 1969 Act were not intended to be punitive.

In spite of this, based upon some observations of the workings of the Juvenile Court in Leeds, an experiment was undertaken which sought to use the court, and its power to adjourn a case, as a means of encouraging school attendance (Berg, 1980). The children taken to court largely fulfilled the criterial of truants as earlier outlined (Berg, Butler *et al.*, 1978). A procedure was adopted whereby children brought before the court were randomly allocated (at the toss of a coin) to one of two groups – those who received supervision orders, and those who faced an adjournment and subsequent recall to court in order to monitor their progress. The research team established that, in the following six months, those subject to the adjournment procedure maintained a 65 per cent attendance record, whilst those placed under supervision maintained a 49 per cent attendance. These results appeared to create a great deal of excitement, particularly among those people who 'appeared' to have little idea that supervision orders tended to be given low priority by social workers. They were taken, by some at least, to indicate the futility and ineffectiveness of social work in general (Brewer *et al.*, 1981).

Encouraged by these initial results the researchers and the magistrates have extended the notion of random allocation in order to test out further what the active ingredients in the courts' activities consisted of and how and why they appeared to produce changes in non-school attenders.

The research, whilst being strongly defended by those concerned (Brown, 1986), has come under sustained criticism on a number of counts. First, there are ethical objections raised about the fact that the court is allocating justice on a random basis, and thereby failing to take on board the requirement, encompassed by the Act, to 'have regard to the welfare of the child or young person'. Second, there are those who question the procedure's legality. The process would seem to be counter to the spirit if not the letter of the 1969 Act. Adjournments, under that legislation, were only to be used to enable further inquiries to be undertaken, or to enable parents to produce further evidence. Finally, it is claimed that the adjournment procedure inevitably results in the serving of more care orders. This in turn means that family life is disrupted; the child is exposed to the *potentially* damaging effects of residential care; and that ultimately the child is not exposed to very much more schooling. The supportive argument here is that moving a child from home, then to an assessment centre, and finally to one or more residential placements is highly disruptive of school life, and likely to expose the child to poor educational experiences. The review of child care law currently being undertaken by the DHSS, may well regularise the situation. It is proposed that local education authorities be deprived of their power to bring care proceedings on the grounds of non-attendance. This would be replaced by the more limited power to seek a supervision order. It is anticipated, in the review, that such supervision should be undertaken by an EWO.

Organisational solutions

A number of organisational responses have been explored as ways of accommodating the non-attending child. They are to be found in a variety of settings and this is reflected in the different rationales which are proffered for their usefulness. SSDs, usually as an alternative to reception into care, may offer IT either on a day or a residential basis. IT developed in response to criticisms about both the effectiveness and the desirability of institutional treatment for children and adolescents. The relatively high cost of residential treatments also played a part in encouraging the search for cheaper alternatives to residential provision. The young person concerned remains at home, apart from sometimes attending weekend activities. He or she becomes part of a group which aims to 'enrich [his] environment and assist with the development' as the DHSS guidelines, published in 1972, put it. What has developed is a rather 'piece-meal' form of provision which mixes activity-based work with various forms of group-work. Within this broad framework various forms of social-skills training and special education may be attempted.

The formal educational system has also responded to the

non-school attender in a variety of ways. Some LEAs have developed a number of 'special units' for such pupils, whilst others have concentrated upon developing a specialist group of staff, and class-room facilities, within the child's existing school. Tutorial groups have been established within some child guidance clinics. These offer a valuable 'half-way' house to the non-attending adolescent, offering half-day attendance as a way of gradually reintroducing the pupil back to mainstream education.

The facts that non-attendance tends to increase among young people as they approach the school leaving age, and that non-attenance is more prevalent in some schools than others are taken as indications, by many people, that the school system itself contributes directly to non-attendance.

A further factor, which has tended to encourage LEAs to move into the area of special provision, relates to the links between poor school attainment and non-attendance. In 1978 the DES published the Warnock Report, which pointed out that some 16 per cent of school children need special education at any one time, and that 20 per cent will require it at some point during their school careers. Consequently special facilities, which focus upon the slow learner or the behaviorally disturbed, have developed as a means of helping the child back into mainstream schooling.

School counsellors and youth tutors

A number of attempts have been made to introduce a greater element of counselling expertise into the formal school setting. To some extent there is the expectation that class teachers are able and willing to offer pastoral care to their students. However, this is inevitably limited by constraints of time and the fact that many teachers have not been exposed to counselling skills training.

The earlier indications that the introduction of specialist counsellors into schools could have positive effects encouraged Rose & Marshall (1975) to establish the Central Lancashire Family and Community Project between 1965 and 1973. This was an action research project which sought to monitor the impact of five school counsellors upon five large Lancashire secondary schools. The counsellors' task was to help children and their parents solve or adjust to personal and social problems. They concluded that 'school social work can reduce the incidence of maladjustment and deviant behaviour to a degree sufficient to warrant the wider deployment of social workers in school.'

Alan Butler attempted to build upon this work by investigating the impact of the short-lived youth tutors scheme within the now defunct West Riding of Yorkshire (Pritchard & Butler, 1975, 1978). Here, too, the results appeared to favour the employment of specialist counsellors, or youth tutors. Demonstrable differences were apparent in both teachers' attitudes towards and perceptions of school non-attendance in those schools with a youth tutor when compared with those that did not have one on the staff.

However, these limited experiments, whilst seemingly successful at reducing truancy levels and measurable maladjustment, have not been widely adopted throughout the school system. In part, this reflects limited financial resources. However, Marshall & Rose in commenting upon the wider applicability of their own findings highlighted what may in fact have been a more important stumbling block. They observed that any further growth in such a service would have to overcome major problems with regard to interdepartmental cooperation and entrenched differences in administrative structures between education on the one hand and social work on the other.

Summary points

- Non-school attendance is subject to a variety of interpretations.
- Unauthorised attendance appears to be quite common, but for most children is only intermittent.
- Three broad categories of non-attenders are commonly identified: truants, school refusers and those withheld by parents.
- Management of the problem begins with a careful descrip-

tion of the circumstances of the non-attendance.
● Intervention is usually a multidisciplinary approach.
● The greater success is likely to be achieved with pupils in the younger age-range who have been identified speedily.

*   *   *

School refusal: a case study

Jasmine was 11 when she started to miss school regularly – particularly at the beginning of the week. She had previously had a reasonable attendance at a smaller primary school which was close to home, but the absences became more persistent on transfer to a larger comprehensive. She complained of feeling sick and having stomach pains. Her mother, who had herself been treated by her GP for depression and 'nerves', became very concerned about this and insisted upon taking her to the doctor and subsequently to a hospital consultant. Nothing organic was discovered.

She was a bright if rather a reserved child who had few friends, none of them of her own age – all younger. An elder sister had been brain-damaged in a car accident and was permanently hospitalised. Her father did not feature very prominently in the family as he worked for an oil company as an engineer and spent much of the year abroad.

The social worker, who was called upon to offer help by the school, noted the following in a case summary: 'Jasmine is an immature girl, with few friends of her own age, who has found problems in adjusting to a new and larger school. Her mother receives little support from her husband, and has to contend with her own anxiety and depression. An older sister, who is severely handicapped, seems to haunt the family and serve as a constant reminder about the dangers of life outside the home.'

Ideally the social worker would have liked to have involved the father in a series of family-orientated sessions; however, this proved to be practically impossible. She therefore undertook six sessions with mother and daughter in an attempt to help them understand how their anxieties were interacting and feeding off each other. At the same time, during discussions with teaching staff, teachers were encouraged to make an effort to integrate her into the classroom and reinforce any positive contributions that she made.

A programme was devised whereby the social worker agreed to take Jasmine to school for four consecutive Mondays. On the remaining days Jasmine's mother was to undertake this with the promise that if she failed for any reason she should contact the social worker immediately.

During the trial period, in spite of a good deal of reluctance on the part of Jasmine and anxiety from her mother, the social worker only had to be called out three times. On each occasion Jasmine complained of some ailment but was taken to school.

On the advice of the social worker Jasmine was encouraged, by her mother, to invite friends back to the house after school for tea.

Regular attendance then resumed. Over the next two years any absences usually followed the ending of a school holiday or return to school following genuine illness. On each of these occasions the school, alert to such possibilities, contacted the social worker. With a display of firmness the social worker was able to effect a return to school on each occasion.

*　　　*　　　*

School refusal: a case study

Sheila was just eleven when she started to miss school. She complained of feeling ill and her mother, initially at least, concurred with this and put her to bed. However, it soon became apparent that there was a pattern to her non-attendance and that this coincided with days on which she had to undress either to do PT or to go swimming. She became extremely tearful and agitated if pressured to leave home, and gradually her mother became drawn into this. She too became tearful and upset at the distress displayed by her daughter. The situation seemed to deteriorate as the problem generalised to other days, and attendance became sporadic eventually ceasing altogether.

Behavioural analysis and discussion with the parents and child indicated more of the picture. Sheila was a bright if overly sensitive only child. Attendance began to deteriorate when she moved to a large school, more distant from home, and when she began to display signs of adolescent maturity. She was apparently self-conscious about her body, and tried to hide this from others including her parents. Sheila's father felt that because she was an only child she was overly close to her mother and had been rather spoilt and over-indulged.

A programme was devised whereby Sheila could be helped to overcome her extreme sensitivity to exposing her body in front of other people. With the help of an educational psychologist she was encouraged to relax and then imagine a series of situations. The imagery was increased in intensity whilst at the same time she was taught to control her anxiety level.

In the meantime the social worker worked with the parents. Their own involvement in the situation was discussed. It was agreed that Sheila's mother try to remain uninvolved in the mornings and that her father should re-arrange his work timetable so that for a few weeks he might take her to school.

Sheila was encouraged not to be so shy about her own body in the house, and the whole family went on expeditions to the local swimming pool.

After some four weeks Sheila's father began to take her to school regularly. Initially this met with some reluctance but his firmness began to produce results. A short contingency programme was drawn up such that Sheila began to be rewarded for days attended, and in particular classes that she went to which involved use of the changing rooms.

*   *   *

Truancy: a case study

John was 14 when he was reported as persistently non-attending. He had had a poor attendance record for some two years but always managed to maintain sufficient days at school so as not to attract too much attention to himself. However, the situation deteriorated and his parents, who previously seemed unconcerned, became alarmed by the fact that he was apparently solvent-abusing with a small group of friends whilst he should have been at school.

He had never been a 'high-flyer' academically and his absences meant that he now struggled to keep up with his class mates. When he did put in an appearance at school he was singled out for comment by his teachers, and ridiculed by class mates. His major interest in life seemed to be playing and watching football. However, this too had been curtailed since his parents had reduced his pocket money, and he was no longer selected for the school team. A system of incentives was drawn up in discussion with John, his parents, and the school teacher. Special efforts were to be made by the school not to pick him out for special attention when he made the effort to attend. However, some extra tuition was arranged so that he might advance more rapidly with his reading which was lagging well behind what one might have expected for his age. His parents were counselled about how they might best get him up and out of the house in the morning, and they were requested to restore his pocket money to its former level. However, he was only to be allowed to attend the local football match if he maintained a full-week's attendance at school. In the meantime social worker and EWO, on a rota basis, agreed to keep a very close eye upon his attendance, so that any lapse could be responded to immediately. The EWO's involvement also served to remind the parents that legal sanctions, were also being considered as a possibility. Within four weeks, with only one lapse when he was consequently prevented by his parents attending a football match, he was maintaining regular attendance.

8

Anorexia Nervosa

Introduction

Earlier in this book, we considered eating disorders which occur mainly in early childhood, and which are usually classified in child psychiatry as 'developmental disorders'. When we move up the developmental scale to puberty, eating disorders which reflect developmental difficulties will have diminished considerably. In the post-pubertal period, however, some adolescents will suffer from anorexia nervosa: a serious eating disorder of increasing prevalence. Unlike the eating disorders of childhood, anorexia nervosa is classified as a 'psychosomatic disorder'. This means that it is a physical disorder in which complex emotional factors play a significant part in the process which causes and sustains the illness.

Anorexia nervosa occurs primarily in adolescent girls who have achieved puberty but, occcasionally, the condition arises before the onset of puberty. In the past twenty years a great deal of research has been undertaken regarding this problem but much uncertainty remains about its causation.

Prevalence

The prevalence of anorexia nervosa is difficult to determine because many sufferers deny that they are ill, while others are hesitant to seek treatment. Kendall *et al.* (1973) studied patients referred to psychiatrists and found an annual incidence of 0.6–1.6 per 100 000 population. A later study by

Crisp *et al.* (1976) examined the incidence of anorexia nervosa in 9 London schools. They found one severe case in every 100 girls attending private schools, but the rate for state schools was much lower. Overall they observed one serious new case for every 250 girls aged 16 and over. Between 90 and 95 per cent of all anorexia patients are girls.

Theoretical models

Cultural factors are relevant to the causation of anorexia nervosa and modern attitudes towards female shape and achievement play a part in the development of the illness. Within Western society there is a noticeable preference for a slim body shape and items on diet and exercise are regular features in many women's magazines. The physical appearance of women is subject to far more public scrutiny than that of men, and the media stereotypes of the slim female seems to carry with it connotations of acceptability, social status, desirability, and power. The misfortunes of the overweight female are, therefore, great, since these attributes are largely denied to her. The only escape from the stigma of obesity is by careful dieting and all women, regardless of their physical make-up, are encouraged to believe that they too can achieve a slim figure. The family acts as a mediator of cultural influences upon its members, and may, therefore, amplify what it sees as desirable qualities and aspirations within society.

Attitudes regarding the physical appearance of women are, however, only a superficial feature of a much more fundamental societal problem. Ideas and attitudes towards women in society are a potent influence upon the ways in which women view themselves. These views are, to a great extent, locked within historical tradition and because of societal concensus, they are accepted as immutable truths rather than ideas or concepts which may be challenged and changed. The 'provider of food' is a role which is primarily assigned to women in society, and is an integral part of the roles of 'housewife' and 'mother'. Ensuring that a family is well-nourished is part of the process of caring, and has become synonymous with the giving of love. This is reinforced by the media representation of women as the smiling and benevolent providers of food. Embodied within such advertising is the notion that women control the dietary intake of family members and that, by implication, they are responsible for the health and well-being of others. Food has therefore become a moral issue, with the wife/mother accepting responsibility and culpability for any deficiencies in diet.

The moral implications of food consumption are also evident in the advertising of products which are not generally associated with healthy eating. Frequently these products (for example, chocolate, cream, etc.), are presented as having particular relevance for women, they are accompanied by advertising slogans such as 'Naughty, but nice' and 'Go on, be a devil', and the 'moral message' is made abundantly clear. Family and wider societal influences upon 'food' and 'eating behaviour' are with us throughout our developmental history, and a disorder such as anorexia nervosa cannot be considered in isolation from them.

Family factors are particularly important, and some authors have suggested that within the families of anorexic patients there has often been a preoccupation with body weight and diet. Moreover, these families are frequently from the middle and upper classes where greater emphasis is likely to be placed upon personnel achievement and success. Individuals within the family will, therefore, be under some pressure to conform to particular rules regarding physical appearance or behaviour.

Interaction between family members has also been linked to the development of anorexia nervosa. Family therapists suggest that anorexic patients play an important role in diffusing conflict within the family. Reported features of these families are their 'enmeshment' (emotional over-involvement with one another), disturbed patterns of communication, and their failure to resolve family conflicts. Often the parents are perceived by therapists to be overprotective, and rigid in their attitudes. They also discourage self-expression and independent activity in their children.

Some studies have suggested a genetic link in anorexia nervosa. The evidence for this comes from studies of families where more than one member has developed the illness, and from twin studies. Anorexia nervosa in identical twins is shown to have a concordance rate of about 50 per cent, while the rate for non-identical twins is about 10 per cent. Because identical twins develop from the same egg within the womb, and share the same genetic make-up, the high concordance rate within this group does indicate that genetic factors may be important in the genesis of the disorder.

Depressive disorders are more common in the families of anorexia nervosa patients, and there is also increased alcohol abuse among fathers. In some cases depressive illness is thought to underlie the anorexic condition, since marked weight loss is an important feature of depressive disorders. Some authors would view both depression and alcohol problems as effective means of withdrawing from situations which are too difficult to face. The situation may be a unhappy marriage, chronic illness in one family member, or some other family problem which is creating stress. It seems fairly certain, therefore, that the family does play an important part in the development of anorexia nervosa, but whether the link is direct, or indirect, is not yet fully understood.

Individual factors are also important to an understanding of the illness. Anorexic patients are known to express conflict regarding their physical growth, sexuality, and independence. For some, these conflicts may be avoided or postponed by retreating into the illness. As the illness becomes more severe menstruation ceases, and the other signs of pubertal development slow down dramatically. The inhibition of pubertal changes is under the control of the hypothalamus (the brain stem), and there is overwhelming evidence for hypothalmic disorder in anorexia nervosa. This slowing down, or halting, of pubertal development has led some authors to suggest that anorexia nervosa is a form of regression to a simpler pre-pubertal state, when the individual can again be dependent upon the parents (Crisp, 1977). Some anorexic girls have very specific fears about sexual development. In therapy, the adolescent may reveal vivid sexual fantasies in which weight gain is associated with pregnancy (Bruch, 1973).

Opinion is divided regarding the personality characteristics of adolescents, prior to the onset of the illness. However, there seems to be a high level of agreement that the potential anorexic is usually compliant, perfectionistic, and dependent in personality. These individuals strive to please others; their feelings of self-worth are highly dependent upon the opinions of others; and they are greatly influenced by external standards of appearance and behaviour. Achievement is, therefore, important to them, since this is one way of ensuring acceptance and approval by others.

Some adolescents may fear a loss of control over their eating and weight-gain, and their symptoms arise as an attempt to establish firm control. A growing sense of control is often accompanied by feelings of achievement, and these may be an important stimulus towards increasingly severe dieting. It is not uncommon for perceptual distortion of the body image to occur in anorexia nervosa. The subject will affirm a continuing need for dietary control, even though she may be quite emaciated in appearance. She views her true body weight in a distorted way, and this provides the rationale for continued dieting. Poor nutrition arising from inadequate dietary intake may be aggravated by vomiting, and the use of laxatives. These activities take a heavy toll on the physical well-being of the individual, and will commonly produce tiredness, physical debility, increased sensitivity to cold, insomnia, and depression.

Anorexia nervosa can be precipitated by traumatic events such as a family bereavement, or family disruption due to marital breakdown. In some individuals the disorder follows a period of physical illness, while in others it may arise in association with increased academic pressures or expectations. Some adolescents say that the illness is just an extension of 'normal' dieting which has 'got out of hand'. Certainly many patients go through a period of mild or occasional dieting before progressing to more rigid and severe food restriction. However, dieting is so common among adolescent girls that it is difficult to determine its exact role in the development of anorexia nervosa.

Management

The management of anorexia nervosa is closely related to the seriousness of the symptoms at the time of referral. There is good evidence to suggest that by the time many anorexics come to the attention of helping agencies, the illness is well established and serious. There are many reasons why subjects and their families delay in seeking treatment, and denial is probably a very important psychological mechanism in this. Parents, and other family members may take some time to recognise that anything is amiss. In some families the anorexic adolescent may be skilled at hiding the problem, or in diverting attention from it. Careful avoidance of carbohydrate-rich foods, missed or unfinished meals, and secret vomiting or purging may go undetected. Some families may have their own reasons for denying that there is a problem, particularly when acknowledging it will raise other conflicts which they would rather avoid.

Sometimes the family will be alerted to the problem by outsiders. People who have only sporadic contact with the subject are sometimes more likely to notice weight loss than those who have daily contact. There may be marked opposition to outside intervention by the adolescent, accompanied by promises and reassurances to the parents that food intake will be increased. Again, this is likely to delay the family in seeking help.

Anorexia nervosa occurring in younger subjects, or where the illness has been of short duration, may respond to out-patient treatment by a psychiatric team (psychiatrist, social worker, psychologist, and community psychiatric nurse). However, since the illness is often well-established by the time referral is made, the majority of cases are dealt with on an in-patient basis in child and adolescence psychiatry units. Bearing in mind the resistance reported in many families referred for help, and the potentially life-threatening nature of the disorder for some individuals, in-patient assessment and treatment is regarded by many psychiatrists as the most appropriate form of intervention.

Once the adolescent has been admitted to hospital, the crucial task is to overcome their resistance to eating. If the illness has become life-threatening because of considerable weight loss, then enforced tube feeding or intravenous 'drip' feeding may be undertaken as an emergency. In order to overcome resistance in therapy, the individual is encouraged to consider weight gain towards the norm for her age and height, but without creating undue anxiety. This is usually achieved through a one-to-one psychotherapeutic relationship, which is frequently combined with a behavioural programme in which rewards are geared to weight gain. A psychiatrist or a social worker will usually initiate the psychotherapeutic relationship, while a psychologist, or nurse, will take responsibility for the behavioural programme. However, these roles are interchangeable between the different members of the psychiatric team, depending upon their knowledge, skill, and experience.

The purpose of psychotherapy is to help the adolescent to leave behind the child-like role they have adopted, and to acknowledge the reality of puberty, and the challenges it poses (Crisp, 1980). The concept of 'change' is introduced to help focus the individual's thinking towards alternatives to her anorexic life-style. This will only be achieved if the relationship provides enough support to prevent her from retreating into the illness in order to avoid the challenge. Careful planning by the team should ensure than the pace of psychotherapy is matched to progress on the behavioural programme so that gains in one stimulate gains in the other.

The combination of a behavioural programme and individual psychotherapy constitutes the first stage of what is likely to become a long and difficult treatment programme. The regular monitoring and maintenance of the adolescent following discharge from in-patient care is crucial, and may last for several years. Social work intervention will be an important feature of both short and long-term management, and this will require skills both in individual and family work. The progress made in hospital will usually provide the basis for continued work with the family. Since the individual is being helped towards 'normal' adolescent development, it follows that the difficulties in adjustment which can arise in this period, must be anticipated and dealt with. The anorexic adolescent is, however, likely to be quite vulnerable, and will require on-going social work support in order to negotiate these difficulties. The parents will also need support if they are to accept and understand adolescent behaviour, and the issues this raises for them.

Many parents have very real worries about adolescence and its potential difficulties, and their own experience of adolescence, as it was for them, will take on a special significance. In retrospect, they may regard their own adolescence as having been a difficult time, during which they made many mistakes and achieved little that was positive. Unhappy memories will often make parents more determined to avoid the same pitfalls with their own children. The result may be a style of parenting which is rigid, overprotective, and which adheres to age-inappropriate methods of child management. Some parents consciously deny their child's obvious physical maturity. They refuse to consider that there will be a time when the child will separate from them, and transfer affection to others outside the family. The social worker will need to demonstrate sensitivity and firmness in tackling issues such as these within the family. This process is made easier when the social worker can create a setting in which parents and child can articulate their need, and look for constructive solutions to their dilemmas.

Family therapists have undertaken interesting and innovative interventions with anorexia sufferers and their families. In many cases they believe that there is little need for in-patient assessment and treatment if a family therapy approach is adopted at the outset. Their analysis of the problem rests upon the initial diagnostic meeting with the family, and the conflicts that this reveals. During the session families are often requested to 'enact' the problem: this requires them to move from describing the difficulty to demonstrating it. To achieve this, a simple meal such as sandwiches and coffee is provided, and becomes the focus for intervention. The parents are asked to encourage and help their anorexic child to eat, and in doing so reveal the overall patterning of relationships within the family. Clearly this can be a very potent means of demonstrating the eating problem, and the family dynamics which may be maintaining it. By the end of the session, the eating problem can be viewed within the context of the conflicts existing between the different family members. Family therapists believe that weight gain will often begin shortly after this diagnostic session, and will be maintained with further family therapy sessions.

It can be seen that the diverse theoretical explanations of the illness have led to equally diverse therapeutic interventions. Most authors are in agreement, however, that the therapeutic approach adopted must address both the eating problem and the underlying family conflict, if improvement is to be maintained.

Outcome

Anorexia nervosa tends to run a variable and unpredictable course, often over several years. Follow-up studies indicate that between 50 and 60 per cent of patients make a full recovery some 4–7 years after the initial onset of the illness. In about a quarter of cases there will be significant improvement but without total recovery of normal functioning. The individuals concerned may continue to exhibit minor eating problems, or difficulties in social interaction and adjustment. However, for some patients (between 20 and 25 per cent) the illness runs a chronic course, leading to continued weight-loss, amenorrhea, and serious social and psychological handicaps. Between 5 and 10 per cent of patients will die, usually by suicide. This significant mortality rate highlights the importance of skilled and sustained medical, and social intervention, in order to prevent a fatal outcome.

Summary points

- Anorexia nervosa occurs primarily in post-pubertal girls, leading to marked weight-loss and amenorrhea; the illness rarely occurs before puberty, and is seldom seen in boys.
- Cultural factors within society produce important and powerful stereotypes of the 'ideal' physical shape; these may exert pressure on adolescents to conform; the family is an important mediator of cultural influences.

● Family communication and interaction are marked by dependency, defensiveness, rigidity, and conflict-avoidance; disagreements often remain unresolved; problems of depression or alcohol dependence may be present in the family.

● Anorexic patients often express conflict regarding their physical growth, sexuality, and independence; the illness may represent a regression to an earlier, less problematical stage of development; weight-gain is associated with sexual fantasies in some adolescents; others fear loss of control over their eating and weight-gain.

● Anorexic patients often have personality traits of compliance, perfectionism, dependence, and over-sensitivity to criticism, prior to the onset of the illness.

● There is some evidence to suggest that genetic factors may be important in the development of the illness.

● Traumatic events such as marital breakdown, bereavement, physical illness, or academic failure, may mark the onset of the illness.

● Management of the disorder is usually undertaken on an in-patient basis; treatment will be a combination of behaviour therapy, individual psychotherapy, and family therapy; long-term follow-up is essential for these adolescents and their families.

*　　　*　　　*

Joanna was 13 when she began to exhibit symptoms of anorexia nervosa. However, a year had passed before her parents sought referral to a child psychiatry unit. The illness appeared to have been precipitated by marital friction, which had culminated in the parents' setting up separate households under the same roof. Joanna's poor eating habits and subsequent weight-loss seemed to have gone unnoticed amid the continuing marital strife. Father occupied an executive position in industry; he worked late and was frequently absent overnight on business trips. Mother worked part-time as a secretary, and Joanna and her younger sister Ruth (9 years) shared the mother's part of the house with her. The seriousness of Joanna's condition became apparent when Father took the girls to Spain for a short holiday. Joanna ate very little at the hotel and vomited after taking food; her sleep was disturbed and she was generally sad and tearful. Father cut short the holiday and the family doctor instigated the referral to child psychiatry.

Following admission to hospital, Joanna was started on a behavioural programme to stimulate weight gain. Initially, she put a lot of pressure on her parents to discharge her, and the social worker had to work hard to convince them of the seriousness of Joanna's condition, and the importance of the treatment programme. This was presented to them as the first of many conflicts they would face with Joanna, and between themselves as parents.

Joanna's weight gain was modest, and she was slow to achieve rewards on the behavioural programme. The parents complained frequently and bitterly to the social worker about what they perceived to be the barbaric and inhuman treatment of their daughter. Since Joanna had not at that stage achieved the reward of having her parents visit her in the unit, they were understandably anxious and angry. Sympathetic listening by the social worker stemmed the tide of anger temporarily, but a more direct intervention was needed to divert their attention from Joanna and her treatment programme.

Joanna's treatment plan was described to them as a three-stage process, having 'beginning', 'middle', and 'end' stages. Each stage would have its attendant difficulties and, to some extent, these could be anticipated. Her admission to hospital had marked her entry into the 'beginning' stage, and this would be completed when her weight reached the designated norm, and was maintained there. The 'middle' stage would begin with her discharge from in-patient care, and her adjustment to living at home again. This stage would be the longest of the three because of the continuing need for support and help over time, before the 'end' stage was reached. This final stage would be marked by Joanna's achievement of 'normal' functioning both at home and in the wider social environment. The social worker expressed the clear expectation that 'conflict' and 'resistance'would be encountered at each of these stages. Having captured the parents' attention and interest by this discussion, the social worker then suggested that the parents should adopt a similar three stage model in considering their current marital situation. This model had particular relevance for the parents since both had stated that their marital relationship would not be resumed, though for convenience they intended to continue their present living arrangements.

In this family, anorexia nervosa seemed to have the dual purpose of diverting attention from the parents' marital problems, while simultaneously uniting them in their concern for Joanna's health. Not unnaturally, the parents were keen to focus upon the illness rather than the underlying difficulties in their relationship, hence their repeated complaints about Joanna's hospital treatment. With persistence, the social worker was able to re-focus their energy into discussion about their marriage, and their plans for the future. The 'beginning' stage for them was the discussion of their marital difficulties, and their joint agreement to a plan of action. They rejected the idea that marital therapy might help them resolve some of their differences, having tried this some years earlier through the Marriage Guidance Council. With reluctance, but also with some relief, they accepted the suggestion that they should discuss plans for a trial separation. This would allow them the option of reviewing their decision at a later stage, and adjusting their plans accordingly. The social worker undertook this intervention in the belief that continuing marital friction is often more damaging to children than a marital separation.

During this time Joanna was maintained on her behaviour programme, and was also seen in individual sessions by a psychiatrist. This enabled her to express some of her anxieties about her parents' marriage, and her fear of 'abandonment' should they decide to separate. After a while she was able to join her parents in family sessions where her worries gained fuller expression and discussion. By this time the parents were into their 'middle' stage: the sorting out of all the personal and practical difficulties that accompany separation. It was notable that, as these family sessions progressed, Joanna's weight gain improved, and she became more irritable and temperamental in her parents presence.

After eight weeks Joanna had reached her 'normal' weight and was allowed to spend weekends at home. Two weeks later, having maintained her 'normal' weight, she was discharged from in-patient care. The family were seen weekly for follow-up appointments during her first three months at home. Joanna's weight was maintained but the parents were now complaining about her rudeness and laziness in the house, and her 'bizarre' make-up and clothes. These developments were discussed in the family sessions, but with only a modicum of acceptance and understanding on the part of the parents. Some setbacks occurred during the following six months, but these were handled without the need for readmission to hospital. Subsequent episodes of weight-loss in Joanna were temporary, and linked to specific stressful events in her life at that time. These were resolved by increasing the therapeutic input over the stressful period, and by the continuing participation of both parents in the therapeutic process.

9
Drug Abuse

Introduction

Drug abuse has, in the last two decades, come to represent a major challenge to the health and welfare services. Reports would suggest that the problem has increased dramatically during this period, and continues to do so. The recent national campaign by the Health Education Council, aimed at informing young people of the dangers inherent in abuse, has occurred in response to the growing concern among political and professional groups, and the public at large.

Drug abuse has a less protracted history than, for example, substance abuse, and was seen to become a serious problem among young people during the 1960s. It arose as part of the widespread popularising of the 'alternative' youth culture which, among other things, advocated the use of various hallucinogenic substances to heighten and distort perceptual experiences. The production and distribuition of drugs in Britain is governed by specific legislation which prohibits their illicit production or importation, and the non-medical use of certain drugs. The legislation carries with it heavy penalties for drug offences, and it gives the police wide powers of enforcement.

Drug abuse, and the deteriorating and depressing lifestyle which is commonly associated with addiction, frequently features in referrals to social workers, whether they be area-based, or attached to specialist units. Frequently referrals will focus upon the unmet needs of children who suffer emotional and physical neglect because of their parents' drug habits.

This may be particularly true for youthful parents who are abusing drugs. The social worker may need to mobilise resources to bring treatment within reach of young people, or statutory child care procedures may need to be invoked to 'rescue' children from backgrounds of serious neglect or physical abuse. The parents of children who are abusing other substances, for example solvents, may also seek advice from social workers regarding the management of the problem.

There is, therefore, a clear need for social workers to be knowledgeable about the specific features of drug and substance abuse. This will enable them to understand the effects of abuse, the problems likely to be associated with this, and the most appropriate method of intervention.

Most drugs cause some degree of dependence, whether this be physical or psychological dependence. Physical dependence means that the user needs to continue taking regular amounts of the drug in order to avoid the unpleasant and painful physical symptoms which accompany withdrawal. The person who has psychological dependence experiences a continuing need for stimulation or pleasure, which is obtained from drug use. Often these individuals will feel unable to cope with life without the support of drugs, and will, therefore, view their withdrawal with anxiety, fear, or panic.

Distinctions between the use and abuse of drugs are socially defined in that drug use is consistent with contemporary social mores, while drug abuse is viewed as deviance from acceptable social standards of behaviour. Drug abuse must also be viewed within the context of a society which advocates and promotes the use of some harmful and addictive substances (for example, alcohol, tobacco), but has clear legal and social sanctions against the use of others. The response of society to drug abuse has been both prescriptive and punitive. On the one hand, medical and psychiatric treatment is available for those who are addicted to drugs, while on the other there exist severe legal sanctions against the sale or possession of illegal drugs. There is, therefore, continuing debate about the position of drug abusers within society – is their behaviour indicative of illness, social deviance, or is it normal behaviour?

Drugs commonly used in abuse

The Misuse of Drugs Act and Medicines Act are the main pieces of legislation governing the manufacture, supply, and non-medical use of drugs in this country. Drugs which are controlled by the Misuse of Drugs Act carry with them increasingly severe penalties for misuse, according to which category they are in. For example, drugs such as heroin, morphine, cocaine and LSD are in Class A, which carries the most severe penalties; amphetamines, barbiturates, hypnose-datives, and cannabis are in Class B; distalgesic, and mild amphetamine-related drugs are in Class C, and carry lower penalties. Minor tranquillisers such as Valium, Librium, and Ativan are not controlled under this Act but are classified as 'prescription only' under the Medicines Act.

1. Heroin and other opiates

The dried milk of the opium poppy contains morphine and codeine, and an extremely potent white powder (heroin) is produced from this. Opiate drugs have important medical uses, and a number of synthetic opiates are manufactured as painkillers. These include pethidine, dipipanone (Diconal), dextropropoxyphene (Distalgesic), and methadone. The powder obtained from both natural and synthetic opiates can be swallowed, or injected in a water solution. Heroin can also be smoked or sniffed. The majority of heroin illegally imported into this country originates from the Indian subcontinent (the 'Golden Triangle'). Compared to other drugs it is relatively easy and cheap to obtain. There can be wide variation in the 'street value' of the drug, and in the quality, since the drug may well have been mixed with similar-looking substances such as talcum powder, flour, or glucose, before being offered for sale. An addict might expect to spend £20 per day in order to support the habit.

The opiates induce feelings of relaxation, drowsiness, warmth, personal well-being, and freedom from anxiety. These sensations will diminish as tolerance is achieved, and the user will then have to increase the dose in order to obtain the same 'beneficial' effects. As tolerance increases, financial problems are likely and the user may become undernourished and unable to maintain a reasonable standard of physical care and hygiene. As with other drugs, intravenous injection maximises the effects of the drug.

Withdrawal of the drug after long-term use, or short-term use involving high doses, will produce varying degrees of physical discomfort. These include muscular spasms, tremor, aches and pains, sweating, shivering, sneezing, and yawning. These symptoms are more pronounced during the first ten days of withdrawal, but feeling of physical debility and fatigue are likely to persist for some months.

2. Cocaine

Cocaine is obtained from the coca plant, which is a native shrub of the Andean regions of South America. It is a powerful stimulant and, like heroin, is sold in the form of white powder. It is usually sniffed through the nose, but can be taken by intravenous injection. The drug is expensive to obtain and its regular use is, to some extent, limited to the higher income groups. Abusers of other drugs may, therefore, make only intermittent use of cocaine. A regular user might well spend over £100 per day on the drug.

Cocaine produces exhilaration, and exaggerated feelings of physical and mental well-being. Paradoxically, the drug may occasionally produce feelings of anxiety and panic, particularly where large doses are used, or where many small doses are taken over a short period of time. It has no significant tolerance or withdrawal symptoms, though there is likely to be strong pshychological dependence. Discontinuation of the drug will produce feelings of lethargy and depression, and these can be a powerful temptation towards resuming use of the drug. Continued use over time will also produce discomfort because of over- excitability, poor sleep, weight loss, and nausea, These symptoms are likely to diminish quite quickly once the drug is discontinued, but feelings of lethargy and depression may persist for some time.

3. Amphetamines

These are synthetic drugs produced for medical use. Illicit production of these drugs is, however, relatively simple, and the frequent availability of large quantities on the illegal market make them easy, and comparatively cheap to obtain. They are produced as tablets or capsules, but can be powdered and mixed with water for intravenous use.

The effects of amphetamines are similar to those of cocaine: physiological arousal, increased energy and confidence, and decreased appetite. Tolerance can be achieved fairly quickly, resulting in increasingly higher doses in order to achieve the desired effects. As energy decreases, the user will experience feelings of exhaustion and depression. Withdrawal from the drug will also produce lethargy and depression, and intense hunger. Consistent high dosage may lead to delusions, hallucinations, and paranoid feelings, and there is an increased risk of damage to blood vessels, and heart failure.

4. Sedatives and hypnotics

These drugs are usually referred to as 'hypnosedatives' and are frequently used in medical practice. They are used on prescription to calm people down (sedatives) or to induce sleep (hypnotics). The most commonly misused drugs in this group are barbiturate sleeping tablets (for example, Seconal, Nembutal, Tuinal). They are usually sold as capsules for oral consumption, but the powdered contents of the capsule can be injected in solution. The injection of sedatives has come to be regarded as the most dangerous form of drug abuse. Most sedatives have been produced for medical use, and those that are available illegally, have usually been stolen from medical supplies.

The effects of sedatives are similar to those of alcohol in that they produce feelings of relaxation and contentment. Heavy doses will, in the main, produce sleepiness, poor control over speech and bodily movements, and clumsiness. In this state the user is at considerable risk of physical injury because of poor concentration, confused thinking, and impaired physical co-ordination. Sometimes the user may become unconscious, and this can lead to respiratory failure, and death, since the difference between an 'effective' and a 'fatal' dose is quite small. With the heavy user who has achieved tolerance, there is a marked and continuing risk of accidental overdose. The use of alcohol in conjunction with sedatives increases the potency of the drug, and escalates the risks involved. Heavy users are also at risk of physical complications such as pneumonia, bronchitis, and hypothermia.

Tolerance and dependence (both physical and psychological) are common in sedative abuse, and withdrawal will produce nausea, sleeplessness, irritability, twitching, fainting, and occasionally, convulsions. Withdrawal from high doses of barbiturates is undertaken gradually, since sudden withdrawal can be fatal.

5. *Minor tranquillisers*

In medical practice, the safer benzodiazepenes (for example, Valium, Librium, Ativan) have largely replaced barbituates in the treatment of anxiety, tension, and poor sleep. They are the most commonly prescribed drugs in current use in the UK, and their medical use is twice as common among women as among men. Their widespread medical use means that there is unlikely to be much of a demand for their illicit production, and their appearance on the illegal market is infrequent.

The benzodiazepenes have a much less intense effect than barbiturates, though they can impair physical and mental activity. As with alcohol, they are likely to produce some disinhibition leading to aggressive or violent outbursts. High dosage will induce drowsiness and sleep, and the use of alcohol will potentiate the effects of the drug. There is a reduced risk of fatal overdose, compared with barbituates, though the risk is increased if high doses of benzodiazepenes are used in conjunction with alcohol.

The long-term use of benzodiazepenes can produce psychological dependence. Physical dependence is uncommon and though withdrawal can produce insomnia, nausea, and anxiety, these symptoms are less intense both in degree and duration, than those of barbituates withdrawal.

6. *Cannabis*

Cannabis, which induces mild intoxication and relaxation, comes from the *cannabis sativa* plant, which is easily cultivated in Britain. The active ingredients are contained in resin which is scraped from the plant and formed into blocks. Herbal cannabis (marijuana) is obtained from the dried leaves of the plant. The drug is most commonly combined with tobacco for smoking, but it can also be mixed with food.

The use of cannabis is widespread and it is probably the most common drug currently in misuse. It can have either a stimulating or a relaxing effect, similar to the effects of alcohol, and this will largely depend upon the mood and expectations of the user. High doses can produce altered states of consciousness with perceptual distortion, and impaired concentration and judgement. It can also exacerbate pre-existing feelings of anxiety or depression in the user.

Long-term smoking of cannabis carries with it the same risks that accompany tobacco smoking (e.g. respiratory disorders, bronchitis, increased risk of lung cancer), but as yet there is no firm evidence for other adverse effects associated with the drug. There is likely to be some degree of psychological dependence, since smoking cannabis can become an established social habit among some groups.

7. *Lysergic acid diethylamide (LSD)*

LSD is a synthetic white powder, usually formed into tablets or capsules for oral consumption. Its use was increasingly popular during the 1960s and early 1970s, but in comparison with other drugs, its current use is rare. The effects of the drug depend very much on the user's situation, his or her expectations, and the amount of drug taken. These include perceptual distortion (auditory and visual), the intensification of colours, sounds, etc., and feelings of ecstasy which are often perceived as being of mystical significance. The drug may also produce unpleasant reactions (a 'bad trip'), in which feelings of depression, dizziness, increased anxiety, and disorientation may be prominent. There are no known long-term physical ill effects and the drug does not create dependency. Regular users may, however, experience brief psychotic episodes, acute anxiety, and 'flashback' phenomena where parts of a previous 'trip' are re-experienced in vivid detail.

Prevalence

The Institute for the Study of Drug Dependence conducted a national study (ISDD, 1973), which also included 70 English schools in its sample. Nine per cent of pupils reported having taken drugs, increasing with age from 6 per cent among fourth-formers to 12 per cent among sixth-formers. Less than half had used drugs on more than three occasions. The most popular drug was cannabis (7 per cent) and about 2 per cent each had used sedatives, stimulants, or LSD. The incidence of cocaine or opiate use was practically nil.

Other surveys undertaken in the 1970s generally confirm that about 10 per cent of school pupils aged 14 years and over have used drugs, with cannabis being most popular, followed by amphetamines and LSD, and with very little abuse of opiates or cocaine. The most recent survey (Pritchard *et al.*, 1986) was carried out in schools in Southampton and Bournemouth, using a sample of 14–16-year-olds. Fifteen per cent of the children reported drug abuse, with cannabis and other non-hallucinogens being most popular (11 per cent). Heroin, cocaine, LSD, and amphetamines had been used by 4 per cent, in addition to the use of cannabis and solvents. The findings from this study lend some support to the view that serious drug abuse occurs as a progression from the use of alcohol and tobacco, to cannabis, and finally to the use of 'hard' drugs such as heroin and cocaine. The authors found that 75 per cent of their 'abuse' sub-sample were smokers, and 82 per cent were involved in under-age drinking.

Students in higher education have been a popular focus for studies in drug abuse. Overall, the results give a range of incidence of 10–40 per cent between different institutions, with cannabis being the most commonly used drug. The incidence of hard drug use within this population is largely unknown since there is much more difficulty in obtaining such data for student populations.

The peak age for drug abuse is between 18 and 25 years. One Canadian study found that half of the sample who were abusing drugs were under 21. Males outnumber females in a ratio of about 4:1, especially among those who become addicted. During adolescence the sex difference are not so apparent, though males are likely to predominate. There is some social class variation in the use of drugs; marijuana use, for example, having been associated with college populations. Financial status affects the use of cocaine, and because of its increasing cost, it has tended to be associated with the upper classes and the higher income groups. The problem of drug abuse is greater in urban than rural areas, and particularly in the inner-city areas.

As the use of drugs has become more widespread, ethnic differences in the populations abusing drugs have tended to diminish, though marijuana smoking is still thought to be more common among blacks than whites. Among the users of hard drugs there are now few racial differences.

Social factors

Peer group influence is thought to be a strong predictor of marijuana abuse (Becker, 1953), though it does not predict the progression to the use of other drugs. Non-addictive drug use is not thought to lead to criminality, though delinquency prior to drug use seems to be a significant factor.

Research has shown that radical or unusual political or religious beliefs are more likely to occur among drug takers. Drug-taking is rule-breaking and deviance from acceptable social norms. It is not surprising, therefore, that non-conformity, less identification with social institutions and conventional values, and rejection of current religious views of man, are all seen as strong predictors of abuse (Jessor *et al.*, 1973). Family influences are also seen as important, and drug abuse is associated with poor parent–child relationships, broken homes, and drug use by parents. Particularly important are those parents whose dependence on alcohol or tobacco, for example, acts as a role model for their children.

There is no single personality or social profile of the young drug abuser but low self-esteem, pessimism, apathy, and depressive moods have all been noted. In addition, rebelliousness, disobedience to authority, and law-breaking are associated with drug abuse, though the abuse may only be a part of a delinquent cluster of activities rather than a discrete entity.

Management

Input from Social Services may be as part of the service of a specialised unit, or from a community-based social work team. Unit attachment is usually hospital-based, the social worker being part of a multidisciplinary team. An important function of such a team would be liaison with community-based workers around issues of case management, coordination of services, and in-service education and training. This function would also extend to school staff, and professionals in other allied services. This would include the expanding voluntary sector of non-statutory services such as drug day centres, community workers, and detached youth workers. During the past few years, community drug teams have been set up in many urban areas. These are multidisciplinary teams usually containing a social worker, psychologist, nurse, and workers from the voluntary sector. The teams work closely with GPs, in-patient medical services, and social services, in order to achieve early identification of drug problems, and to co-ordinate community resources in the management of drug abuse. The community drug teams also undertake a vital role in the education and training of other professionals, and in raising public awareness of drug-related problems within their own locality.

In establishing any treatment or rehabilitation service for young people, there will always be conflict between the individual drug misuser's rights, particularly his right to confidentiality, and the wider interests of society which encompass both the legal protection of the community, and the maintenance of adequate health standards. Individual workers must, therefore, manage the dilemma of meeting the needs of the individual through a confidential and trusting relationship, while recognising the need for order and control within society at large. Strang (1984) has pointed out that individuals whose lifestyles and behaviour do not differ markedly from 'normality' are now being drawn into the expanding drug sub-culture. Many drug abusers do not suffer from dependence nor do they experience associated medical problems from drug misuse. Others do experience serious problems, and may also be suffering from an underlying psychiatric disorder. The response, therefore, is always an individual one, matching the needs of the individual to the resources available.

It has been argued (Yates, 1985) that energy should be directed more towards the support and expansion of non-specialist services, since over-emphasis on the importance of specialist drug treatment units must undermine, to some extent, skill and confidence which has been built up in the former. This is particularly true when considering the increasing number of drug problems which are dealt with in the voluntary sector. Official statistics are usually based on abusers who have been notified or self-referred to medical authorities (the 'dependent' group), and do not, necessarily, take into account the vast numbers of mainly 'experimental' and 'recreational' users who are contained within society.

Yates emphasises the importance of determining, albeit crudely, the type of abuse (experimental/recreational/dependent), the primary and secondary problems associated with the drugs in use, and the way in which these complex factors serve to maintain and stabilise the habit. Drug abuse may, therefore, be regarded as a 'normal' habit which has become 'out of control'. He stresses that any therapeutic response must relate in an individual way to the 'effects' of the drug, the 'situation' in which it is used, and the 'expectations' of the user. This approach focuses on the social components of the behaviour whilst simultaneously acknowledging the physical (medical) aspects of addictive behaviour. He argues that failure to do this serves only to perpetuate the mystique of drug abuse as an arcane and bizarre piece of behaviour which can only be remedied by sophisticated and highly specialised therapeutic units.

Field social workers would find much to agree with in this approach since many forms of drug abuse are handled by them outside of the 'specialist' framework. This does not decry the value of such units, rather it argues for a more realistic community based approach which recognises the contribution of non-specialist workers, and their continuing need for support, guidance, and consultation, by the 'experts'.

A number of treatment approaches have been described in the literature, utilising hospital-based and community resources, and both individual and group therapy models. The majority of writers are in agreement that the starting point of intervention, whatever the therapeutic setting, should be a thorough assessment of the meaning of drug abuse in the individual's life. For the adolescent this would also include an assessment of the family and their use or abuse of substances; parenting style and the disciplinary skills employed; and any inconsistencies in parental attitudes or behaviour regarding drug use.

The age of the drug abuser is also of relevance. Research seems to indicate that younger adolescents use drugs in imitation of their parents, for the excitement of doing the 'forbidden', or in response to peer group pressures. With older adolescents there are often overtones of defiance towards family or societal pressures, feelings of anger, or a desire for brief escape from anxious or depressive feelings. There is, therefore, a need to understand the reinforcers for drug abuse, so that intervention will have specific goals.

The initial aim of intervention is the progressive building of confidence and trust in the individual, so that he will have some resources to cope with the later, more challenging, aspects of therapy. Bratter (1973) has described a four-stage treatment plan which utilises direct procedures and behavioural techniques, rather than psychotherapeutic methods:

● The therapist seeks to *establish a therapeutic alliance* by considering the obstacles to treatment; this exchange allows the adolescent to voice his fears and anxieties, assesses his motivation, and allows him to test the limits of therapy.

● The therapist uses *forced behavioural change* to reduce the abuse to a less debilitating level; this demanding and directive strategy reveals the rational self-interest of the individual, or lack of it, in wanting to change; the support and encouragement of other family members may need to be enlisted at this stage, to maintain the pressure for change.

● The therapist attempts *reorientation and reconstruction of behaviour* by challenging the adolescent to exercise control over his negative responses; by considering the options available, the therapist demonstrates that present solutions are inadequate and that only continuous self-searching can lead to new choices.

● *Growth and development* are fostered by setting goals, usually via a contract, in which the adolescent takes a crucial role in monitoring current performance, and planning future goals.

Other approaches advocate the use of family contracts which focus on the associated problems of drug abuse, so that the adolescent's identity does not solely revolve around him being a drug abuser. This approach is regarded as being particularly useful with clinic defaulters, where trained community workers can pursue treatment goals in the home setting. Again the approach is behavioural, using a hierarchy of increasingly difficult tasks for the adolescent and the family to focus upon.

Motivation is clearly an important consideration in any programme of intervention, but it is likely to be a major deficit in serious drug abusers who are referred for help. They will often present with many adverse factors in their current life situation and be unable to perceive the links between depressing social circumstances, and their drug abuse. If motivation can be increased then work can begin. Failing this, serious consideration must be given to the need for inpatient assessment and treatment. Individuals who experience serious withdrawal problems will also require in-patient services, if they are to have any chance of reducing reliance on drugs. In-patient units can offer continuous medical supervision, and opportunities, using individual and group methods, to increase self-esteem and to rebuild the patient's life within a structured and supportive environment.

As with many other forms of social work, professional involvement with the problems of drug abuse must address itself to the broad legal framework within which both the problem and the helping agency exist. The possession and abuse of certain drugs is a criminal offence and the police have a duty to impartially enforce the law when transgressions are discovered. For social workers employed in community-based services these legal sanctions may appear unhelpful because they can so often disrupt and impede ongoing work with drugs offenders. These young people are unlikely to discard the habit spontaneously and, regardless of social work involvement, they will remain at risk of arrest and prosecution. The growing concern over the Acquired Immune Deficiency Syndrome (AIDS) and the vulnerability of some drug users to this disease has created additional concerns. For example, it has been suggested that the spread of the disease may be curtailed by the free provision to drug abusers of new hypodermic syringes, in exchange for used ones. But the police have the power to stop and search individuals they suspect of drug abuse, and the possession of drug-injecting equipment would very likely lead to arrest and prosecution.

The legal difficulties of working with drug abusers extend also to issues of 'care and control'. Care proceedings may be the last resort for those young adolescents who persistently abuse drugs to the detriment of their own health, well-being, and safety, and where parents are either unable or unwilling to exert control. In addition, young pregnant women who abuse drugs run the risk of having their babies removed to local authority care at birth if there is evidence that maternal drug abuse has adversely affected the baby's health.

The problems for social workers in working within the strictures of the law emphasise the need for effective consultation and liaison. This should not be solely at the monitoring and policy-making level, but also in the day to day management of the social, medical, and legal issues in individual work with clients.

Summary points

- Drug abuse is a serious problem which affects many adolescents, both males and females. The incidence rises with age, the peak age being between 18–25 years. Problems of serious addiction are more common among males.

- Drugs are mainly classified in terms of their potency, tolerance level, and addictive qualities. Reference is often made to 'hard' drugs (for example, heroin, cocaine) which are highly addictive and physically debilitating; by comparison, 'soft' drugs (for example, cannabis, minor tranquillisers) are considerably less harmful.

- Drug abuse must be viewed within the wider context of a society which has variable standards regarding the use of addictive substances. Some are socially acceptable (for example, alcohol, tobacco) while others are prohibited.

- Problem drug-taking arises from diverse sources. Important influences are the availability and cost of drugs, peer group pressures, and factors within the family. Some families may (a) encourage drug abuse by example, or (b) motivate the individual to reject parental standards and guidance, and to use drug abuse as a form of rejection or rebellion.

- The equivocal status of some of the addictions has influenced the professional response to drug-related problems. There are arguments for having both community-based services and specialised units offering in-patient care. Each service emphasises its own combination of social/adaptive or medical/illness models in the management of problems.

*   *   *

Luke referred himself to the SSD following his eviction from a privately rented bed-sit because of rent arrears. At 18, he was now homeless, unemployed, and beset by many personal and social worries. He had been sleeping rough for a week, but at the time of referral was sharing a squat in a semi-derelict house with three other men.

In his early teens Luke had frequently been in trouble with the police because of petty crime, glue-sniffing, and under-age drinking. His anti-social behaviour, coupled with regular truancy, led to continuing friction at home. At 17 he eventually left home and went to London to look for work. He stayed in London for a year, during which time he was introduced to heroin use. During his first few months in London he worked unofficially as a barman in a gay club, but as his use of heroin increased, so his efficiency at serving the customers decreased, and he lost the job. For much of this time he lived with various acquaintances who sub-let accommodation to him.

His experiences while working at the club led him to believe that he could support himself by becoming a rent boy, and he pursued this with some trepidation. During the next six months his heroin-use increased, and he became less-discerning about the punters he propositioned on the streets. One evening he was savagely beaten by two men he had picked up in a pub. He was found by the police and admitted to hospital with moderately severe injuries. While he was in hospital, he was offered the opportunity of transferring to a drug dependence unit for treatment, and he accepted. He discharged himself from the unit after a month and returned to Manchester.

On his return, he made no contact with his family, and instead stayed with various friends and acquaintances around the city. Constant financial hardship led him back to prostitution, but with less success than he had experienced in London. By chance he met his married sister one day and she persuaded him to stay overnight with her. It was pressure from his sister that led him to seek help from Social Services.

Initially, the social worker had to undertake a good deal of practical intervention with Luke to help him find accommodation, and to sort out his financial situation. His sister's influence seemed to have given him some motivation for change and the social worker capitalised on this by seeing him often during the first two weeks. Hostel accommodation was obtained through a local voluntary agency which offered a counselling service for young drug-abusers, and Luke began to attend their twice-weekly support group.

With Luke's permission, the social worker contacted his sister and explored with her the supports available in the family, and the potential difficulties Luke would have in the future. A major difficulty for those involved in Luke's rehabilitation lay in the continuing temptation for him to return to his old haunts where he would be at risk for further drug-abuse. In part, this was remedied by creating opportunities for him to be involved in more worthwhile pursuits (for example, helping out at the day centre, attending adult literacy classes to improve his reading and writing skills, and encouraging and helping him to complete job applications). His sister was also able to take a very active part in Luke's life by arranging regular contacts with him at her home. This also enabled her to reintroduce him gradually to other family members, and to enlist their support. She was successful in securing some temporary work for Luke via one of his brothers-in-law, and as a result, he began to view the future with more optimism and a greater degree of self-esteem.

10
Substance Abuse

Introduction

The term 'substance abuse' is most commonly associated with solvent abuse, though many different kinds of substance may be involved. The abuse of substances is not a recent phenomenon. In ancient times a variety of substances were used in many different cultures to achieve states of euphoria, disorientation, and depersonalisation, often to give added significance to ritual or religious gatherings. Pioneer work in the field of anaesthesia during the eighteenth and nineteenth centuries led to the introduction, and subsequent abuse of, such substances as nitrous oxide (laughing gas), ether, and chloroform. Current concern over substance abuse by young people perhaps obscures the fact that such abuse has been quite widespread since the early 1940s (Barnes, 1979). In the early 1950s there were many reports from the USA of young people inhaling gasolene fumes. In the late 1950s and early 1960s reports began to appear of young people increasingly using solvents for inhalation.

The most popular form of substance abuse is glue sniffing, but substances such as paint thinner, dry cleaning fluid, nail-lacquer remover, petrol, and anti-freeze, may also be used for inhalation. Another method of abuse is the inhalation of aerosols by direct spraying into the mouth. Substances such as butane gas, hair spray, furniture polish, deodrants, and 'damp start' sprays for cars, are frequently used. This is a particularly dangerous method of abuse since direct inhalation of aerosol products can cause sudden death by laryngeal spasm.

The most common methods of inhalation are by direct sniffing from a container, or by decanting the substance into a polythene bag and placing this over the mouth and nose. Others will saturate clothing, rags, or a handkerchief, in order to inhale the toxic vapours. In addition to these mehods, some individuals will place a ploythene bag over the head to reduce oxygen intake, and thus potentiate the effect.

The effects of inhalation are similar to those of alcohol, and occur very quickly, usually within minutes. The substance can have both a stimulant and a depressant effect, and responses will vary according to the type of substance, the amount used, and the physical stature of the individual. The stimulant effect is characterised by excitability, loud and aggressive behaviour, impaired judgement particularly regarding personal safety, and poor coordination of physical movements. Hallucinations are said to be common. Some users may show behaviour similar to that produced by the use of sedatives. The effects are of relaxation, drowsiness, inattention, dizziness, lethargy, and slurred speech.

Regular use will produce unpleasant physical symptoms which may be readily apparent to the onlooker. The individual will appear pale and lethargic, with skin irritation and sores around the mouth and nose. Users will also suffer inflammation of the eyes and throat, together with nausea, headaches, and diahorrea. Heavy use can lead to temporary loss of consciousness. In addition to physical symptoms, heavy users are likely to suffer a deterioration in their personal standards of hygiene, and will present as apathetic and lacking in interest. Substance abuse can also be detected by staining of clothing through spillage of the products used, and by the smell of volatile substances on the breath and clothing.

There are conflicting views as to the long-term or fatal effects of substance abuse, although 116 deaths occurring in 1985 were connected with solvent misuse. It is important, however, to differentiate between the direct effects of the substances used, and the situational variables which may increase the risk of a fatal outcome. Research evidence does suggest that the long-term use of some substances will produce damage to the brain, liver, or kidneys, and even short-term use is likely to damage the delicate membranes in the throat and nasal passages. Anderson (1982) has reported on a number of deaths following substance abuse and found these to be almost equally divided between the use of aerosols (inluding butane gas), and various solvents. Deaths occurring as a direct effect of the substances used were caused by asphyxia, anoxia, cardiac failure, and pulmonary and respiratory failure.

The circumstances in which the abuse occurs, however, do contribute to the likelihood of death occurring. Individuals who use a polythene bag over the head are placing themselves in danger of suffocation, particularly if the abuse occurs when there is little likelihood of help being available in an emergency. Abusers who become comatose may well die through inhalation of vomit while in this state. Accidental death may result from disinhibited and reckless behaviour, or the disorientation which often accompanies intoxication. Because substance abuse is commonly regarded as anti-social behaviour, it tends to be undertaken in locations which are likely to be isolated from potential sources of help (for example, derelict houses, waste ground, open countryside). These dangers are obviously greater for the solitary abuser, rather than for those who undertake it as a group activity.

Prevalence

Substance abuse occurs primarily in the 12–17 age range, and is more common among boys than girls. Some recent studies have suggested that the sex difference is now less marked, and that girls are increasingly turning to solvent abuse. Approximately 17 per cent of 12–17-year-olds will have abused solvents at some time in their lives, and within this age group about 2 per cent will currently be abusing these substances. The incidence decreases with age so that in the 18–25 years age group the rate for lifetime use is around 10 per cent with approximately 1 per cent being current solvent abusers. A recent study by Pritchard *et al.* (1986) found that among an 'abuse' group of 14–16 year olds, 4 per cent were abusing solvents only. A further 4 per cent, however, were abusing solvents in addition to the abuse of other drugs. This gives an overall prevalence of solvent abuse in 8 per cent of this age group, and is consistent with the findings from several other studies.

Personal and social factors

There are a number of background factors associated with substance abuse, though these are by no means definitive and must, therefore, be regarded with some caution. Research evidence suggests that many substance abusers have a poor self-image, and frequently experience feelings of low self-esteem. This is most marked in those young people who do not discontinue the habit after a period of experimentation, but go on to become regular users. Other studies have shown that marital disharmony, family stress, and the break-up of families, are important features in the backgrounds of abusers. Such adverse factors present a depressingly familiar picture to social workers, and are a feature of other kinds of referral which come their way (for example, delinquency, running away from home, deliberate self-harm). Substance abuse may, therefore, offer to many young people an exciting, but temporary, escape from their depressing home circumstances.

There is little evidence to suggest that personality functioning in abusers differs from that of non-abusers. The relationship between abuse and other aspects of personality is difficult to determine, since the abuse cannot be regarded in isolation from the cluster of anti-social behaviours of which it is usually a part.

Management

Much of the research on substance abuse has produced tentative, and to some extent, speculative findings, which reflect for some writers an over-emphasis on the medical, rather than social, aspects of the phenomenon (Asquith & Jagger, 1985). This development is seen to have clear political implications in terms of the 'labelling' and 'control' of the behaviour. At the same time it has created a problematical status for substance abuse which is confusing to both professionals, and parents, and has increased the difficulties surrounding intervention. Substance abuse is not a criminal offence, nor are there any direct legal sanctions against it. There are, however, indirect legal sanctions as, for example, when crimes are committed while under the influence of some intoxicating substance. Young people may, therefore, be detained by the police because of disorderly behaviour, damage to property, or a breach of the peace following substance abuse. This has led to occasional calls within the media for legal sanctions against the sale and abuse of various substances. Other writers voice the counter-argument that to 'criminalise' the activity substantially increases its mystique and attractiveness to vulnerable young people, leading to an escalation of the behaviour.

Is substance abuse a problem? If it is, how should the problem be defined, who should define it, and what if any intervention should be offered? Certainly, when compared with other forms of abuse, such as tobacco and alcohol use, substance abuse does not achieve a very high priority rating. These are questions which perplex many professionals who are expected to adopt an interventive role in relation to substance abuse, but for whom confusion and uncertainty are significant features of their professional response. Parents expect, and often demand, intervention to stop their child's substance abuse. Social workers are often the recipients of such demands but, having made an assessment of 'the problem', they often have no clear idea of what their professional responsibilities are in the matter. The problem, therefore, frequently rests with the police who, though they have no specific legal powers regarding substance abuse, frequently find themselves escorting intoxicated youngsters back to their homes with stern comments and advice.

In a recent review, Prins (1985) comments that 'Like many problematic behaviours, substance abuse provides a fertile ground for the protestations and activities of the treatment zealot.' Various 'treatment' approaches are described in the literature, all of which utilise some form of individual or group therapy, but with varying degrees of success. Most authors are in agreement that in the initial stages of intervention, an individual approach is likely to be the most acceptable, and productive form of therapy. O'Connor (1983) has described the running of a clinic which was specially set up to offer a therapeutic service to substance abusers. Important features of this service were:

● an 'open' clinic taking referrals and self-referrals in an informal, non-statutory setting;
● the clinic makes regular use of volunteers and 'recovering' substance abusers in their therapy sessions;
● great importance is attached to the initial contact; the reception group is geared towards giving peer support and fostering positive adolescent identification;
● after the reception meeting, the adolescent is given individual counselling which leads, after a few sessions, to membership of a counselling group.

The individual sessions are geared towards helping the adolescent feel relaxed and comfortable with the counsellor, so that trust may develop. Once trust is established, counselling will become more challenging. Self-observation is encouraged so that the adolescent will become aware of the effects of substance abuse on his physical well-being and appearance. The overall aim is systematic reduction of substance abuse, but without the use of negative sanctions. Group sessions offer encouragement and support to members by showing how other members have made a step by step recovery, and how they have managed to maintain a substance-free lifestyle. Special attention is given to the psychological factors and likely withdrawal symptoms, and to creating or expanding other satisfying life experiences. The process is both educative and therapeutic, and other family members and professionals are mobilised to offer support and continuing encouragement. At various stages practical advice on health, hygiene, and diet is offered, and all participants are encouraged to seek a medical check-up.

The setting up of a service such as this seems to offer a good deal of promise to young substance abusers by addressing both the medical and the social factors involved, and within a non-threatening and supportive environment. Field social workers, by virtue of their education and training, would have the group work skills necessary to begin such a venture, and to draw in other interested professionals. The position of residential social workers is rather different since they have day-to-day responsibility for the management of young people in Care. In the past their have been many reports of solvent abuse sweeping, like an epidemic, through residential establishments. Staff can often feel isolated in dealing with such problems, and community resources may offer little support to them in their daily management of abusing youngsters.

Thompson (1982) has outlined some strategies which he has found helpful in managing the problem in residential settings. He advocates an approach which aims on the one hand to reduce the availability of substances within the locality, and on the other hand to respond to the direct physical effects of substance abuse. Staff can take local action to try and control the sale of products to young people, and liaison with local shopkeepers can reduce both the sale and theft of abusive substances. The unpleasant physical effects of substance abuse often disappear quite quickly once the practice is discontinued, and this is seen as a useful incentive in motivating residents towards change.

Summary points

- Substance abuse is a general term referring to the inhalation of a variety of products which, initially, produce feelings of elation and excitement. Solvents are the most commonly abused substances.
- It is usually a group activity, and is more common among males than females. Within a group of abuses, the habit may continue for some months before being discontinued voluntarily. More prolonged abuse is likely to occur among solitary abusers.
- The visible signs of abuse include inflammation of the skin around the nose and mouth, and irritation and soreness to the eyes. In addition, the smell of products may be

detected because of spillage and staining of clothing. Loss of appetite, nausea, and listlessness are also common.

● The anti-social 'image' of substance abuse means that it is often a secretive activity, undertaken in isolated locations. The true incidence of the behaviour is, therefore, difficult to determine.

● Substance abuse is not a criminal offence, but the police may become involved either because of local concern, or through the detection of crimes committed by intoxicated youngsters.

● Social workers are often required to assess and manage substance abusers within the community. The problem initially requires an individual approach, later moving to the use of group work skills, and family intervention techniques.

*   *   *

Gary (14) was seen at the SSD at the request of his mother. He had a three month's history of glue-sniffing which was said to have stopped a month earlier. During the previous week Gary had been found unconscious on the kitchen floor at his grandmother's house with a large, open tin of floor adhesive beside him. He was admitted to hospital but was discharged after 24 hours. It appeared that Gary had tried to stop the habit but without success, and he had become more secretive in his glue-sniffing. In the main, he was undertaking this at his grandmother's house while she was out in the evenings.

Both mother and son appeared well-motivated towards professional social work intervention, and following assessment, a plan of action was agreed. Initially, Gary was seen three times a week for individual counselling, and the parents attended the department weekly for supportive counselling. Though the parents were legally separated, the father was persuaded to attend since Gary still held him in high regard. After two weeks, Gary joined a small group of adolescent boys meeting weekly at the department. Two of the boys shared a glue-sniffing problem, and the other three were each subject to Supervision Orders from the Juvenile Court.

Social work with the parents was both educative and supportive. They were given factual information about solvent abuse and were able to discuss this in relation to Gary. Father needed a lot of encouragement to stay involved since he regarded his role within the family as peripheral. He no longer lived with the family, visited infrequently, and saw his parenting responsibilities as having ended with the marital break-up. The importance of his function as a role model for Gary, and as a support to his wife in carrying out the responsibilities of parenting was re-emphasised at each session. The social worker was able to help the parents to work out how they would monitor and manage Gary's behaviour, and what practical steps they might take in diverting him from further solvent abuse. For example, they needed to balance their surveillance of his outside activities with Gary's need for some independence and freedom, without accusing him or provoking unhelpful confrontations with him. They were also encouraged to think of ways of increasing positive parental contact (particularly with father), around social activities. This involved quite limited goals initially, because of the need to gradually accustom the parents to working together, even though they lived apart.

11
Attempted Suicide

Introduction

During the last twenty years there has been a dramatic increase in non-fatal suicidal behaviour among adolescents, especially deliberate self-poisoning. The available statistics show that this increase began in the late 1960s, continued throughout most of the 1970s, but began to tail off in the early 1980s. Since then the number of non-fatal suicidal acts has remained fairly constant, and some reports have even indicated a slight decrease in the statistics. Nevertheless, suicidal behaviour among adolescents continues to present a major challenge to the Health and Social Services.

The assessment of suicidal behaviour in the young has become an important issue for social workers, more so since the recent publication of the DHSS guidelines to Health Authorities on the assessment and management of the problem. The relative absence of formal psychiatric disorder within this patient group, coupled with the clear evidence of adverse social factors, has re-emphasised the importance of social work intervention. Recognition of this is embodied in the DHSS recommendation that local authorities should appoint a social worker to deal specifically with the problem of attempted suicide. It is envisaged that the establishment of these posts will be an effective means of building up both a therapeutic resource and a training resource, and will form the core of a multidisciplinary service.

Prevalence

Both attempted suicide and completed suicide are rare in children under the age of 12 years, though suicidal thoughts, threats, and actions occur in 10 to 30 per cent of children aged 6–12 years referred to psychiatric services. There is general agreement in the research that female attempters greatly outnumber males, usually in the order of 4:1, and that this is more marked in younger patients, and in those who overdose rather than use other methods of deliberate self-harm. Rates for attempted suicide in girls increase rapidly from age 12 to 16, and continue to increase into the early 20s. Suicidal behaviour is less common among boys, especially under the age of 14 after which it increases gradually with age until well into the 20s.

Vulnerability factors

The literature on adolescent suicidal behaviour has indicated that adolescents who deliberately harm themselves may be particularly vulnerable to such behaviour because of a longstanding history of problems of varying degrees of seriousness. The behaviour and attitudes of parents and other family members are of importance here, as are the more overt signs of marital failure and family breakdown. Disturbed family functioning and the stress that disordered interaction produces have long been associated with behavioural and emotional difficulties in childhood and adolescence. Commonly the problem is one of continuing conflict between parent and child,. often presenting as a series of disciplinary crises which fail to be resolved.

In some families, parents may be largely unavailable to their children in any real emotional sense, and this may be particularly stressful for adolescents who are attempting to meet a variety of developmental tasks and issues in an environment which is both unsupportive and insensitive to their needs. Emotionally detached parents make their children feel unwanted and unloved. They are not available as a resource in times of stress and thus cannot satisfy the child's dependency needs. It is not unexpected, therefore, that many youngsters should respond to this continual frustration of their dependency needs by becoming angry and aggressive. Where hostility and aggression are turned away from the parents and employed inwardly against the self, the adolescent may display intense depression, a tendency towards self-abasement or self-injury, and may carry out suicidal wishes. In some families role-confusion, or role-reversal between parent and child is common and this is thought to impede or distort the normal process of adolescent adjustment. Children who take on a parenting role in response to their own parent's child-like dependency may well feel 'trapped' in an untenable situation not of their own making. A suicidal act may serve as a desperate, but effective, means of escape from this difficulty for the child (Kerfoot, 1979).

Many studies point to the pervasiveness of family breakdown in the backgrounds of young people who attempt suicide. Broken homes due to the separation or death of parents are common, more so than in other adolescents referred to psychiatric services. Parental loss due to continuing marital discord and poor relationships is particularly important since divorce or separation may well hurt a child more than the death of a parent. A childhood characterised by this is associated with attempted suicide in subsequent years. Previous suicidal behaviour among other family members is frequently found, and there is often a history of psychiatric illness in the parents.

Some authors have linked child abuse with adolescent suicidal behaviour, suggesting that parental assault, rejection, and scapegoating are important contributory factors. Parental behaviour of this kind is thought to produce feelings of worthlessness, badness, and self-hatred in the child. Facilitated by low self-esteem and poor impulse control in the child, self-hatred is effectively transformed into self-destructive behaviour. Recent reports propose a link between sexual abuse and adolescent suicidal behaviour (Anderson, 1981).

Low self-esteem and a lack of investment and involvement in family life are important factors in adolescent suicidal behaviour because many of these young people complain of feeling isolated or alienated in relation to their family. In these situations communication appears to have broken down, there is less flexibility and openness, and the adolescent may resort to actions rather than words in order to communicate distress. In addition, poor standards of parental supervision and guidance may have resulted in the child being particularly vulnerable for impulsive ways of responding to stress. Communication may improve in some families following an episode of suicidal behaviour, but in others it will remain unchanged, or may deteriorate further.

Other factors, such as delinquency, previous suicidal behaviour, poor school record, unemployment, periods in care, and running away from home are reported with consistency in the literature on adolescent suicidal behaviour. The presence of these factors may serve to enhance the adolescent's negative self-concept so that she more easily takes on a negative role in relation to her family, and to life in general.

Although only a minority of adolescents involved in suicide attempts are found to have a major psychiatric disorder, depressive symptoms are common, and are often combined with feelings of hopelessness. However, the relationship between depression and suicidal behaviour is complex. While many young suicide attempters complain of depressive symptoms, the converse is not true. Moreover, it remains unclear whether or not these 'depressed' youngsters have a major psychiatric illness, or are suffering from transient symptoms associated with often untenable psycho-social situations. In some older adolescents the picture may be complicated by problems of alcohol or drug abuse. Physical ill-health prior to making a suicide attempt is frequently reported and as many as half of these adolescents will have seen their family doctor in the month preceding their attempt (Hawton *et al.*, 1982a).

These individual and family factors may well increase the vulnerability of the adolescent to subsequent stress, especially when they occur in combination rather than individually. In addition there may be wider social factors at work which would increase the stresses experienced by young people. Some of these (for example, rising unemployment) are readily discernible, but others are less easy to identify. In a general sense they are often regarded as elements of breakdown within the social and moral fabric of society, or the inappropriateness or obsolescence of some of our social institutions, and the alienation which may stem from this. Much depends upon the individual concerned, and their personal resources and resilience in negotiating these difficulties. Failure to do this successfully can shake the confidence and well-being of a young person, and thereby increase vulnerability.

Precipitating factors

Suicide attempts in adolescence most commonly follow quarrels with parents or with a boy- or girl-friend, though often in the setting of more longstanding personal or social difficulties. Many adolescents report an accumulation of difficulties, often during the preceding 12 months, and the stress associated with these creates vulnerability in the individual. In such circumstances, a precipitating event (for example, a quarrel, or a disappointment) may easily provoke an impulsive response in the adolescent. The explanation for this may be that the event is perceived by the adolescent as an insurmountable obstacle, help is either unavailable or unrecognised by them, and they may entertain the belief that a solution cannot be found.

Methods and motivation

Between 80 and 90 per cent of adolescents admitted to hospital following a suicide attempt will have taken an overdose of tablets. Attempts involving more violent means of self-injury are more common among boys than girls, and are usually associated with a greater degree of suicidal intent. Impulsivity is a marked feature of overdosing in adolescents, and the episodes often occur when there is a strong likelihood of the event being discovered quickly. There is likely to be little evidence of premeditation but, where this does occur, then it is usually within the previous 24 hours. The majority of younger adolescents obtain their tablets from home where there is often little difficulty in gaining access to them. More than half of the suicide attempts in the under 16 age group are likely to involve the use of prescribed medication, while the use of analgesics and paracetamol occurs in approximately a third of this group (Kerfoot, 1984). Though there is often little danger to life from the substances used in overdosing episodes, the children themselves would not necessarily be aware of this, since the power of the drug is, for them, an unknown factor. A younger adolescent or child may consume only a small number of tablets in the belief that their use is dangerous, or potentially fatal. Others may consume large quantities of paracetamol, in the mistaken belief that they will quickly recover from whatever damaging effects the drug will have. The use of paracetamol in overdose has resulted in the unintended death of some adolescents, because of the profound liver damage caused by the drug.

The motives for suicidal behaviour in adolescents are often complex to unravel. A study by Hawton and colleagues in Oxford (1982b) suggested that adolescents view their overdose as a means of gaining relief from a stressful state of mind or situation, and as a way of showing other people how desperate they were feeling. They suggest that the appeal function of overdoses by adolescents is usually interpersonal rather than directed towards an outside helping agency. In some cases there is also a strong suggestion that the behaviour is aimed at seeking retribution from parents, or changing the behaviour of significant others towards the adolescent. For adolescents who have experienced an accumulation of stressful problems in the recent past, the suicide attempt may serve as a means of 'escape' or of gaining 'breathing space' for a while. Others may see it as a positive act of control over a life which seems woefully out of control. It has been suggested that previous suicidal behaviour among other family members, or friends, may offer a precedent to adolescents, who then model their behaviour on those around them. Similar claims have occasionally been made for presentations in the media which portray suicidal behaviour in young people. These issues are difficult to substantiate, and to resolve, and the best we can say is that where there is evidence of previous suicidal behaviour among family members or the peer group, then this simply makes the possibility of indulging in similar behaviour more available to the adolescent.

Assessment

It should now be clear that one of the main features of suicidal behaviour in the young is the family context in which it occurs. The other family members, and particularly the parents, are crucial to the assessment of suicidal behaviour and the formation of management of plans. The whole process of assessment should reflect care, concern, and a willingness to invest time and effort into the exercise. Time is of the essence, and the speed with which one is able to mobilise resources to meet the demands of the situation may well determine the therapeutic success, or failure, of the entire venture. Experience would suggest that the 'crisis' and immediate post-crisis period are the times during which the most profitable work can be achieved. It is important, therefore, that the adolescent should be seen for assessment as soon as she is medically fit for this. Early assessment allows a clearer understanding of the circumstances and the motives associated with the attempt, and also reduces the likelihood of rationalisation or distortion of the facts by parent or child. It is self-evident that the assessment cannot be regarded as carrying very much weight unless it has involved both the child and the parents (or parent substitutes).

The setting in which the assessment takes place may also influence the degree to which it can be carried out with satisfaction. Some children are admitted to hospital, others are not. Some are seen on medical wards, or in a psychiatric unit, while others may be assessed at a later date either on an out-patient basis, or by another community agency. Some children may fall through the net altogether if, for example, the parents refuse hospital admission and then avoid all further contact with the social worker.

The styles and routines of assessment are many and varied, and have in the past been influenced mainly by the availability of psychiatric help. However, the increasing number of admissions of suicidal adolescents to hospital has meant that psychiatric services have become overstretched. A positive development from this has been the increasing use of personnel from other disciplines (for example, social work and nursing) in the assessment of suicidal behaviour. Several evaluative studies have demonstrated that both social workers and nurses, with appropriate training, can safely and reliably assess suicidal behaviour.

The initial assessment may be carried out on an individual basis with the adolescent and parents having separate interviews followed by a family interview, or it may be conducted as a series of family interviews from the outset. With some families there may be clear contra-indications for using a conjoint family interview and the social worker would need skill and sensitivity in order to recognise when this was the case. For example, conjoint interviews are often counter-productive if there is a conspiracy of silence, if the adolescent hesitates to speak freely unless alone, and if the family cannot focus productively on the problem.

The assessment procedure

The general purpose of the assessment is two-fold: firstly, to collect accurate data from the client(s) so that decisions arrived at with them, are achieved in an informed and appropriate manner; secondly, in engaging and sustaining the clients in interview, the social worker is also assessing their interest, motivation, cooperation, and capacity for change. In the case of suicidal behaviour, the social worker will focus the assessment interview in order to address a number of pertinent issues concerning the current episode, and the likelihood of further suicidal behaviour occurring. Once an initial rapport has been established, the assessment will cover the following:

- *Circumstances*: the suicidal episode, drugs used, availability, source, liklihood of discovery, suicidal communications, motives, precipitants, previous suicidal behaviour.
- *Social life and activities*: out of school activities, peer group network, casual/close friendships, dating, leisure activities, degree of freedom from parental authority/intrusion.
- *School*: time in school, changes of school, attendance, work, and behavioural records.
- *Problems and coping strategies*: current problem be-

haviour, worries, fears (for example, delinquency, truancy, running away, alcohol/drug abuse, etc.), coping skills, ability to locate and use sources of help.

- *General health*: previous significant medical/psychiatric problems, present health status, regularity of contacts with family doctor, clinics, hospitals, and current treatment.
- *Family structure and relationships*: marital status of parents and composition of family; reconstituted families; rating of marital relationship and child's relationship with each parent figure, and with sibs. Current disharmony – frequency and duration.
- *Family circumstances*: environmental problems, housing, unemployment, low income, delinquency. Physical/psychiatric illness or handicap, suicidal behaviour. Extent and use of contacts with social agencies.
- *Contract formulation*: conjoint interview following appraisal and discussion of individual interviews. Formulating the nature and extent of current problems, and possibilities of therapeutic intervention.

Management

Management is related to the degree of suicidal risk present in the case, the likelihood of further suicide attempts, and the availability of supports within the adolescent's immediate social situation. If there is evidence of serious psychiatric disorder, then the child may be transferred to an In-patient psychiatric facility for further observation and treatment. In those cases where there is no psychiatric disorder, but the risk of a further attempt seems probable, then placement may have to be made through Social Services if there are substantial reasons for not returning the child home. For example, some parents may be unable or unwilling to provide the support and supervision which might greatly reduce the risk of a further suicide attempt. In other situations, the child may be beyond parental control, and a danger to herself.

There is a difficulty here for professionals, since pressure of numbers for hospital beds indicates that early discharge from hospital is crucial once treatment for the toxic effects of the drug ingestion has been completed. Pressure is exerted in two directions. Firstly, towards admission into a child psychiatric unit if such a resource is available, and secondly, reception into Care. Both these settings carry with them the problems of stigma and labelling, and the professional capacity for making decisions is often hampered because of the volatile interaction between parent and child. If the child cannot be discharged home from hospital but has to be placed elsewhere, then this should be as part of a considered therapeutic strategy, rather than a temporary expedient. Social workers will inevitably find themselves caught up in this conflict, but without the influence or resources which might empower them to allow the child to remain within the 'neutrality' of a medical ward for a longer period of time.

Even the effects of short-term hospitalisation, however, can influence the future behaviour of the adolescent. Admission to hospital guarantees high attention, and the vast majority of young suicide attempters are always admitted to hospital. Hospital admission may act to reinforce or stabilise the suicidal behaviour so that it is positively, rather than negatively, connoted. This may be particularly true for the less behaviourally disturbed adolescent who would find inpatient care more emotionally satisfying than would a demanding, unruly, and uncooperative adolescent. The conforming and less-troublesome adolescent may be more likely to repeat the suicide attempt if the experience of hospitalisation had proved particularly gratifying for them. They might also be more susceptible to the labelling and stereotyping of their behaviour, once placed in a strong dependency position by hospital staff, and incline towards absorbing these influences rather than resisting them.

An important but complex factor here would be 'treatment', since this would go some way towards addressing the problems created by admission, as well as the problems which led to the suicide attempt. Treatment will often take the form of short-term, intensive social work intervention, but because of the variability of provision, the effectiveness of intervention is difficult to evaluate. Intervention ought to help in these situations but we are not certain that it does so. In addition, where treatment is being offered to children and younger adolescents, then there may be the additional problem of having to overcome parental reluctance and resistance to follow-up.

For many young people and their families, therapeutic help begins while the child is still an in-patient, and continues after the child is discharged from hospital. The form this help will take is based on a careful analysis of the problems presented by the child and family at the time of admission. A major decision relates to the individual or group upon which the intervention will focus, and the form this will take. There are possibilities for various types of therapeutic input, and these are described in detail elsewhere (Kerfoot, 1986). The family context in which adolescent suicidal behaviour occurs suggests that a family approach in treatment may be particularly appropriate. Social work experience with this group of clients certainly indicates that direct work which aims to explore family dynamics and to facilitate more productive interaction, is an extremely profitable way in which to utilise the time available. A family therapy approach can address itself to the difficulties in relationships (both overt and covert), and can ensure that the suicidal behaviour is acknowledged and understood by all those concerned.

In some circumstances it may be more appropriate to see the adolescent, and the parents, on an individual basis. For example, some family members may feel too vulnerable to 'open up' in a family session, and will resist efforts made in that direction. Adolescents who have been striving unsuccessfully towards independence may regard family therapy as yet another, but perhaps more subtle and devious, form of parental control. This can be a difficult situation to manage since some parents will try to push the social worker into a punitive and authoritarian role. This then becomes the vehicle for all their angry and aggressive feelings toward the adolescent, but channelled through the social worker. In such circumstances there would be clear indications for seeing the adolescent individually, or perhaps combining individual sessions with occasional family sessions.

Even the prospect of being seen individually, however, will raise fears in some adolescents about their ability to cope with an interview. The end result may be sullen, uncooperative

behaviour from the adolescent, or even open hostility towards the social worker. Clearly some adolescents require
help to overcome their reluctance or resentment, so that they
can begin to develop trust and confidence, and a positive view
of their own capabilities.

With younger children their ability to participate in 'talking
therapy' may be quite limited, and the social worker will need
to use play techniques in order to engage the interest and
confidence of the child. Play is the natural medium of the
child, and children can often express themselves more
spontaneously through actions rather than words. For example, a game involving the use of family dolls, or a painting, can
become a vehicle for exploration of the child's ideas and
attitudes regarding her life experiences.

Whatever the treatment approach adopted, there are
several points which deserve emphasis. Firstly, timing is
crucial to the entire process of intervention. There is little
evaluative research in this area but our experience would
suggest that whatever the therapeutic aims may be, the social
worker stands the best chance of achieving these if work can
be undertaken quickly and intensively. In many of the
situations we see, the suicidal behaviour has been an impulsive response to a particular crisis. In like manner, treatment
has often utilised crisis intervention techniques to meet the
problem. These are particularly useful in dealing with the
immediate impact of a suicide attempt upon the individual
and the family, but they also serve to establish a basis for
more long-term work, if this seems appropriate. By failing to
respond quickly and purposefully to suicidal behaviour, the
worker runs the risk of 'losing' the family altogether. At the
time of the attempt anxiety and motivation are usually high,
and the opportunity this affords for positive crisis-work
should not be missed. After the initial crisis, families can very
easily lose interest, and draw a veil of secrecy over the whole
episode, if the professional response has been tardy or
delayed.

A further point has to do with motivation. This is an
important issue whenever intervention is planned, but with
children and adolescents, it takes on a very specific importance. The dangers of failing to treat depressed or suicidal

children simply on the grounds of their poor motivation are obvious. There are, however, many young people who, following a suicide attempt, give a superficial impression of disinterest or poor motivation towards therapeutic intervention. This would need careful exploration and assessment if it was to be properly understood. It might be that lack of cooperation or poor motivation on the part of the adolescent is more indicative of her feelings towards her parents, than to her own need or desire for help. In some situations, the friction which produced the suicidal episode will continue unabated during the period of hospital admission, and may even be made worse by the adolescent's behaviour. In such circumstances, one might reasonably expect the adolescent to be uncooperative, unintersted, and rejecting of offers of help, and for their energies to be channelled mainly into the continuing family conflict. Parental apathy or ambivalence may also be an important factor, since this may quickly communicate itself to the adolescent, and induce negative thinking with regard to professional help. Younger children in particular, may be especially vulnerable to, and influenced by, parental attitudes and opinions regarding intervention. They may, therefore, decline offers of help if this is the spoken or unspoken parental message picked up by them.

The effects of treatment with these groups of children and adolescents are difficult to determine since few evaluative studies have been undertaken. No one method of intervention – individual, family, or group – can therefore be reliably preferred over another since the evidence to support this is sadly lacking. What studies there have been seem to show that the young people most likely to stay involved with treatment are those with psychiatric symptoms (for example, depressive feelings, appetite loss, sleep disturbance) at the time of initial assessment. Other follow-up studies have produced findings very similar to those from studies of suicidal behaviour in adults. These indicate that though intervention is helpful in promoting problem-solving skills, increasing personal confidence and social adjustment, it does not alter the pattern of reoccurrence of suicidal behaviour. The rate seems to remain the same whether the individual has received help or not.

Outcome

Findings from follow-up studies indicate that many adolescents experience some improvement in their personal well-being and relationships during the year following their suicidal episode. Predictably, those adolescents who have long-standing family and social problems, together with behavioural difficulties of their own at the time of admission, do least well at follow-up. Repetition of suicidal behaviour during the year following the original episode, occurs in between 10 and 20 per cent of subjects. The majority of repeat episodes happen during the first few months.

Summary points

● Suicidal behaviour is a serious problem affecting children and adolescents. Suicide attempts rise with age, and are more common after the age of 12 years, and occur mainly among girls. Completed suicide is quite rare in the younger age groups, and is more likely among boys than girls.

● The majority of suicide attempts in the young occur as a result of drug overdosage. Attempts involving other methods of self-harm are less frequent, and are more closely associated with boys.

● Suicide attempts are usually precipitated by arguments with parents or peers, or as a result of sudden or unexpected disappointment or loss. In over half of the cases there will be a background of long-standing personal and social difficulties, with an accumulation of problems during the previous 12 months.

● Marked evidence of social disadvantage, as indicated by broken homes, financial insecurity, unemployment, etc., is common. There is likely to be a relatively high proportion of previous psychiatric illness and suicidal behaviour among other family members.

● Assessment can be reliably carried out by appropriately trained social workers. Assessmenmt must involve both the child and parents if it is to be effective in the formulation of intervention plans. This must be undertaken as soon as possible after the suicidal episode.

● The management and treatment of suicidal behviour involves the use of individual and family therapy, together with play therapy or small group therapy. Timing is crucial to the success of any interventive strategy, and individual and family motivation must be carefully assessed and monitored throughout.

*   *   *

Denise (14) and Julie (13) were both admitted to hospital following an overdose of tablets. At the time of this episode, both girls were living in a small children's home, Denise having been in Care for 2 years, and Julie for 9 months. The overdose occurred following a disagreement with one of the residential social workers. For the two weeks prior to the episode both girls had repeatedly arrived late from school, and had gone missing for quite long periods at the weekends. Their explanation for these absences was unconvincing, and they were kept under closer observation from then on. It was soon discovered that the girls had been regularly visiting the house of Julie's mother which was only a short distance from the school. They appeared to have open access to the house whether Julie's mother was there or not. The house had achieved some notoriety in the neighbourhood because of prostitution, and police 'drugs' raids. Both girls found their secret visits to the house exciting since they were able to smoke and drink, and eavesdrop on the various adult conversations taking place.

The visits of Julie and Denise to the house were discovered when the police called there in the course of other inquiries. Denise was prohibited further visits to the house and Julie was only allowed to visit her mother under supervision. Denise became angry and abusive over this, and stormed off to her room with Julie in tow. A short time later, another child reported to staff that both girls had taken some tablets and were lying on the bathroom floor. They were taken to hospital for emergency treatment, and were detained overnight. They had taken 7–10 paracetamol tablets each, and these had been obtained from a staff member's bag.

The assessment was undertaken jointly by the duty psychiatrist and Denise's social worker from the area team. It appeared that Denise had originated the idea of the overdose, and that Julie had gone along with this as a measure of her friendship and solidarity with Denise. On reviewing Denise's history, it appeared that she had been in a vulnerable state for quite some time. She had come into Care following the death of her mother, and her father's hasty marriage to a woman Denise did not care for. Denise's behaviour deteriorated to the point where the rejection and hostility towards her from her parents, necessitated a separation. After six months in Care her parents moved to a town 90 miles away, and for Denise this indicated their continuing rejection of her. The visits to Julie's home, though happy and exciting, had reawakened for Denise her conflicts about parents and children, and her sadness regarding her own future.

Previously, Denise had been quite resistant to attempts by her social worker to explore the past with her, but the crisis of the overdose provided an excellent opportunity for this to be tried again. An overall therapeutic plan was worked out in which Denise's current and past anxieties were linked to constructive plans for her immediate, and her long-term future. A good deal of work was directed at helping Denise to understand how unresolved grief feelings towards her natural mother had exerted a profound and continuing influence upon her life since then. After a month, Denise felt able to tolerate a short visit from her father, and she was also allowed to make short, planned visits to Julie's home. Progress with Denise was slow, and not without setbacks, since her anger and hostility were often explosive and unpredictable. After six months, however, she was spending occasional weekends with her father and stepmother, and they in turn were including Denise in their future plans.

*   *   *

Christine was 11 when she was admitted to hospital following an overdose of 5 Valium tablets. On admission she appeared miserable and withdrawn, but anxious to return home as quickly as possible. When she was told that a social worker would be seeing her mother that same day, she seemed visibly relieved, and became much more responsive to the ward staff.

Discussion with Christine and her mother revealed that they were in a role reversal situation, Christine having assumed much of the responsibility for family and household matters, while mother displayed a child-like dependency upon her young daughter's management skills. Christine was the second born of four children and problems within the family had become acute following the birth of the youngest sibling. Mother had been ill during the pregnancy; it was a difficult birth, and she felt depressed and unwell for many months afterwards. Christine began to help mother by looking after the baby, and over the years her coping skills were gradually extended into other areas of home life. Father had always had a peripheral role within the family and there was constant friction because of his drinking, and his refusal to look for work.

On two occasions in the past, Christine had assumed sole responsibility for management, these having occurred when her mother was admitted to hospital for short periods of psychiatric treatment. On another occasion her mother was admitted to hospital because of an overdose, and subsequent social work involvement proved helpful to the family.

At the time of Christine's overdose, family problems were acute. Her father had become increasingly violent towards mother, there were continuing financial worries, and Christine felt overburdened by all the responsibilities she had taken on. Christine easily obtained the tablets from her mother's room, and took them while she was at school. Admission to hospital removed her temporarily from the role-reversal and brought in social work help from outside. Initially, the social worker took on some of the active parenting responsibilities to give mother the chance to re-learn her role, and to re-establish herself in it. This required almost daily contact from the social worker in order to support mother, and to keep up the pressure for change. Gradually, mother's capacity for making decisions began to improve and her reliance upon Christine decreased.

Individual work with Christine enabled her to give up her mothering role without feeling too guilty or anxious about her mother. Christine had been detained in hospital for two weeks following her overdose, and this separation created a crisis in which change could be promoted. If Christine had not been detained in hospital, then there would have been less motivation for change and a greater likelihood of them resuming the status quo. As mother's confidence and self-esteem began to improve, so the social worker began to devote some time to father and his particular problems.

12
Conclusion

The aim of this book has been to acquaint the busy social worker, whether they work in a residential or in a community setting, with some of the common problems of childhood and adolescence. We have, furthermore, indicated how simple practical advice and assistance may be offered to both the child and their family.

The problems faced by children are currently very high on the social work agenda. However, it is our belief that too often attention is given only to the statutory aspects of such work, to the relative neglect of important emotional and behavioural difficulties that the child may display. In discussing this with area-based social workers, lack of time is usually advanced as the reason for this. The need to monitor children for both physical and sexual abuse dominates many caseloads. But, it is also possible to discern what could be described as a 'skills gap'. Too many social workers are, in our experience, well able to describe a pathological family situation, or a behaviourally disturbed child, but quite unable to frame a suitable intervention. They have had only the briefest exposure to such problems on their basic qualifying course and are then left to sink or swim with woefully inadequate supervision. Supervision, when available at all, tends to be concentrated upon the bureaucratic practices of the department and the scrutiny of travel expenses forms.

Meanwhile, colleagues in hospitals and clinics have in recent years been developing new skills and techniques, new ways of working, based upon a growing body of research based knowledge. We have tried to reflect these important shifts of emphasis, with regard to the management of child and adolescent problems, in this text.

First among these changes has been the growth of family therapy. Much of this stems from the work of Ackerman and his concern that treatment should focus upon the whole family, rather than the individual child. Next, among many changes, has been the growing sophistication of behaviourally-based methods of intervention. These have emanated from clinical psychology, but, as we have demonstrated in a number of our case studies, may be easily applied to general social work practice. The attractiveness of such techniques has been underlined by recent research evidence which either supports these methods or counters commonly heard criticisms. Such evidence includes the realisation that childhood and adolescent disorders are extremely sensitive to the environment, hence lending support to the idea that children should not be treated in isolation from their everyday world. Attempts should be made to alter the functioning of the social system and not just the child itself. Finally, the frequently cited criticism of behavioural therapies, namely that symptom substitution occurs, may be finally laid to rest. It has been held by many people, particularly those of a psychoanalytic persuasion, that because behavioural treatments 'ignore the underlying problems' it inevitably follows that as one symptom is eradicated another develops to replace it. For example, upholders of this point of view would claim that if bed-wetting ceases, after treatment with a pad and bell system, then because the 'real' problems have not been addressed the child concerned will soon start to display some other difficulty – day-time soiling, or school refusal for example. However, the best evidence now available to us does not support this belief.

Because the emphasis has shifted away from the child to the social system that it inhabits, it follows that residential or in-patient treatments are of less significance than they once were. This challenges what has been called either the 'Garage Syndrome' or the 'Doorstep' model of treatment, whereby the parents arrive with the child so that it can be 'fixed' whilst they depart without becoming involved in the process themselves. Increasingly, as we have illustrated, good practice demands parental involvement. In some cases this may mean parental training or the engaging of parents as co-therapists.

All of these changes, by implication, would suggest that the boundary between specialist and generic social workers should begin to disappear. Specialist workers increasingly work with families in their own homes. Meanwhile generic workers should be familiarising themselves with some of these newer techniques so that they are able to refer to, liaise with, and work co-operatively with colleagues, and attempt some of the techniques on their own. Too many social workers seem to adopt an undifferentiated case-work model of intervention without completing an adequate assessment, and without considering what alternatives they might have to offer. Kraemer (1987) has recently pointed out the almost secretive nature of many social work interventions. Social workers must grow in confidence so that they are able to describe and justify exactly what they do. In failing to do this they expose themselves to what may be unjustified criticism.

Finally, it has always been our belief that a social work training, once completed, is only the beginning of a social worker's education. In order to consider themselves as professionals they have an obligation to develop their own skills and keep up to date with recent developments and shifts in knowledge. This is not always made easy by SSDs, many of whom have shamefully neglected post-qualifying training.

Too often it is left to the individual social worker to piece together their own training packages. This means, in many cases, seeking out short courses to attend, trying to update their reading, or forming mutual support and training groups informally with colleagues. Much of our own work, in recent years, has been in assisting with these developments. We stated at the beginning of this book that we thought that it would prove useful to those undergoing initial training. We hope that there is sufficient of interest here to whet the appetites of, and, generate some enthusiasm among, those who wish to develop their knowledge and skill further. We have been at pains, throughout this book, to signpost the way forward by means of pointers to the appropriate literature. Education is a lifelong task and not one confined to childhood and adolescence.

Further Reading

1. Introduction

There are a number of useful introductory texts in the field of child and adolescent problems, for example, Rutter (1975), Wolff (1981), and Barker (1979). The book by Lask & Lask (1981) takes a closer look at the role of social work, but mainly from a family therapy perspective.

2. Childhood problems – the social work context

For a more detailed view of the range of therapeutic possibilities within social work see Brown & Pedder (1979), Boston & Szur (1983), Gorell Barnes (1984), and Hudson & Macdonald (1986). The excellent book by Brenda Hoggett (1981) clearly summarises the complicated field of children's legislation.

3. Eating and sleeping problems

Two books, both by Douglas & Richman (1982, 1984), convey a wealth of interesting material and practical advice, in a very readable form. They focus primarily upon these problems as they appear in younger children, and help in both understanding and responding to these difficulties.

4. Some problems of toileting

The book by Kolvin, *et al.* (1973) contains much useful information on various aspects of these problems, and on their management and treatment. An interesting paper by Sluckin (1975) gives a detailed account of one type of social work intervention.

5. Emotional problems

The clearest introduction to behaviourally based interventions is that provided by Hudson & Macdonald (1986).

6. Anti-social or conduct disorders

Some of the other books in this series, including those by Walker & Beaumont (*Working with Offenders*, 1985) and Jeffs & Smith (*Youth Work*, 1987) should prove of interest. The book by McAuley & McAuley (1977) in our view, provides the best guide to interventions.

7. School problems

An excellent critical overview of the area is provided by Galloway (1985). The collection of papers edited by Hersov & Berg (1980) also contains much useful material.

8. Anorexia nervosa

Crisp (1980) provides a valuable insight into the clinical features of this disorder, and its treatment. For a more broadly based feminist perspective, see the very interesting book by Lawrence (1984). The book by Erichson (1985) gives a vivid and penetrating insight into the impact of anorexia nervosa on the family. The author is the mother of an anorexia sufferer.

9. Drug abuse

The collection of papers edited by Beshner & Friedman (1979) emphasise the problems and dilemmas of working with young drug abusers, and give a comprehensive introduction to the field. Young (1971) presents a wider sociological analysis of drug abuse, using, 'deviance theory' and the 'societal reaction' perspective.

10. Substance abuse

Prins (1985) provides a short, but concise introduction to the growing literature in this field. In her recent book, Watson (1986) takes a reasoned and unsensational view of solvent abuse, analysing both its historical roots and the contemporary social context in which it occurs. For some graphic and tragic case studies of substance abuse see O'Connor (1983).

11. Attempted suicide

The collection of papers edited by Stuart & Wells (1981) give a useful introduction to the subject. Hawton (1986) presents a rigorous review of the literature, and offers useful information on the assessment and aftercare of adolescents. The book edited by Diekstra & Hawton (1986) contains interesting papers on causation, assessment, therapeutic intervention, and prevention.

Some Useful Addresses

National Association of Young
People in Care (NAYPIC),
Maraner House, 28–30
Moseley St, Newcastle upon Tyne
NE1 1DF (091 261 2178)

Anorexic Aid, The Priory Centre,
11 Priory Road, High Wycombe,
Buckinghamshire

Institute for the Study of Drug
Dependence (ISDD), Library and
Information Service, 1–4 Hatton
Place, Hatton Garden, London,
EC1N 8ND

Parents Anonymous, 7 Park
Grove, Off Broadway, Worseley,
Manchester.
(A voluntary organisation set up to
help parents of drug abusers.)

Families Anonymous,
88 Caledonian Road, London N7
(Information on existing parents'
groups, and advice on setting up
similar self-help groups regarding
drug abuse.)

First Key (The Leaving Care
Advisory Service). Offices in:
  Leeds (0532 443898)
  Birmingham (021 328 7296)
  London (01 378 7441)

The Women's Therapy Centre,
6 Manor Gardens,
London, N7

TRANX – Tranquillizer Recovery
and New Existence, 17 Peel Road,
Wealdstone, Middlesex, 1A3 7QX

The Samaritans, 17 Uxbridge
Road, Slough, Middlesex.
(The Samaritans have a National
Youth Officer.)

Basic leaflets for parents on drug and
solvent abuse are available from:
Department DM, DHSS Leaflets
Unit, PO Box 21, Stanmore,
Middlesex, HA7 1AY

Bibliography

Anderson, H. R., Dicks, B., Macnair, R. S., Palmer, J. C. & Ramsey, J. D. (1982) 'An investigation of 140 deaths associated with volatile substance abuse in the United Kingdom, 1971–1981', *Journal of Human Toxicology*, 1, 207–21.

Anderson, L. S. (1981) 'Notes on the linkage between the sexually abused child and the suicidal adolescent', *Journal of Adolescence*, 4, 157–62.

Ashton, M. (1982) *Drug Abuse Briefing*, Institute for the Study of Drug Dependence (ISDD), London.

Asquith, D. & Jagger, E. (1985) 'Glue sniffing – politics of certainty', in Lishman, J. (ed.) *Approaches to Addiction*, Kogan Page, London.

Bakwin, H. (1961) 'Enuresis in children', *J. Paediatrics*, 58, 806–19.

Bandura, A. (1977) *Social Learning Theory*, Prentice Hall, New Jersey.

Barker, P. (1979) *Basic Child Psychiatry*, Granada, London.

Barnes, G. E. (1979) 'Solvent abuse: a review', *Int. J. of the Addictions*, 14, 1–26.

Becker, H. (1953) 'Becoming a marihuana user', *Am. J. of Sociology*, 235–42.

Bellack, A. S. & Hersen, M. (1977) *Behaviour Modification: An Introductory Textbook*, Williams & Wilkins, Baltimore.

Bellman, M. (1966) 'Studies on encopresis', *Acta Paediatrica Scandinavica*, Supplt 170.

Berg, I. (1980) 'Absence from school and the Law', in Hersov, L. & Berg, I. (eds) *Out of School: Modern Perspectives in Truancy and School Refusal*, Wiley, Chichester.

Berg, I., Nichols, K. & Pritchard, C. (1969) 'School Phobia – its classification and relationship to dependency', *J. Child Psychol. Psychiat.*, 10, 123–41.

Berg, I., Butler, A., Hullin, R., Smith, R. & Tyrer, S. (1978) 'Features of children taken to Juvenile Court for failure to attend school', *Psychol. Medicine*, 8, 447–53.

Beshner, G. M. & Friedman, A. S. (eds) (1979) *Youth Drug Abuse: Problems, Issues, and Treatment*, Lexington Books, Lexington, Mass.

Boston, M. & Szur, R. (1983) *Psychotherapy With Severely Deprived Children*, Routledge & Kegan Paul, London.

151

Bratter, T. E. (1973) 'Treating alienated, unmotivated drug-abusing adolescents', *AM. J. of Psychotherapy*, 27, 4, 585–98.

Brewer, C., Morris, T., Morgan, P. & North. M. (1981) *Criminal Welfare on Trial*, Social Affairs Unit, London.

Brown, D. & Pedder, J. (1979) *Introduction to Psychotherapy*, Tavistock, London.

Brown, I. (1986) 'Adjournment: the answer to truancy', *Community Care*, 28 August, 16–17.

Bruch, H. (1978) *The Golden Cage*, Open Books, Shepton Mallet, Somerset.

Crisp, A. H. (1980) *Anorexia Nervosa: Let Me Be*, Academic Press, London.

Crisp, A. H., Palmer, R. L. & Kalucy, R. S. (1976) 'How common is anorexia nervosa? a prevalence study', *Brit, J. Psychiat.*, 128. 549–54.

Diekstra, R. & Hawton, K. (1986) *Suicide in Adolescence*, Martinus Nijhoff, Dordrecht.

Douglas, J. & Richman, N. (1982) *Coping With Young Children*, Penguin, Harmondsworth.

Douglas, J. & Richman, N. (1984) *My Child Won't Sleep*, Penguin, Harmondsworth.

Erichson, A. (1985) *Anorexia Nervosa: The Broken Circle*, Faber, London.

Essen, J. & Peckham, C. (1976) 'Nocturnal enuresis in childhood', *Devel. Med. Child Neurol.*, 18, 577–89.

Farrington, D. (1980) 'Truancy delinquency, the home and the school', in Hersov, L. & Berg, I. (eds) *Out of School*, Wiley, Chichester.

Freud, S. (1977) *Case Histories: 1. Dorn and Little Hans, Penguin Freud Library* (vol. 8), Penguin, Harmondsworth.

Galloway, D. (1985) *Schools and Persistent Absentees*, Pergamon, Oxford.

Gorell Barnes, G. (1984) *Working With Families*, Macmillan, London.

Graham, P. (1977) 'Possibilities for Prevention', in Graham, P. (ed.) *Epidemiological Approaches in Child Psychiatry*, Academic Press. London.

Hawton, K. (1986) *Suicide and Attempted Suicide Among Children and Adolescents*, Sage, Beverly Hills.

Hawton, K., O'Grady, J., Osborn, M. & Cole, D. (1982a) 'Adolescents who take overdoses: their characteristics, problems, and contacts with helping agencies', *Brit. J. Psychiat.*, 140, 118–23.

Hawton, K., O'Grady, J., Osborn, M. & Cole, D. (1982b) 'Motivational aspects of deliberate self-poisoning in adolescents', *Brit. J. Psychiat.*, 141, 286–91.

Hersov, L. (1977) 'School refusal', in Rutter, M. & Hersov, L. (eds) *Child Psychiatry: Modern Approaches*, Blackwell, Oxford.

Hersov, L. (1985) 'Faecal soiling', in Rutter, M. & Hersov, L. (eds) *Child and Adolescent Psychiatry: Modern Approaches*, 2nd ed., Blackwell, London.

Hobbs, S. & Forehand, R. (1977) 'Time out: a review', *J. Behav. Therapy and Experimental Psychiatry.*, 8, 365.

Hoggett, B. (1981) *Parents and Children*, Sweet & Maxwell, London.

Holman, D., Butler, A. & Berg, I. (1982) 'The outcome of encopresis following in-patient treatment', *J. Psychiat. Treatment and Evaluation*, 4, 185–90.

Hudson, B. L. & Macdonald, G. M. (1986) *Behavioural Social Work: An Introduction*, Macmillan, London.

Jeffs, T. & Smith, M. (ed.) (1987) *Youth Work*, Macmillan, London.

Jessor, R., Jessor, S. L. & Finney, J. (1973) 'A social psychology of marihuana use: longtitudinal studies of high school and college youth', *J. Personal. Soc. Psychol.*, 26, 1–15.

Jones, R. (1981) 'Intermediate treatment, research, and social policy', *Journal of Adolescence*, 4, 339–52.

Kendell, R. E., Hailey, A. & Babigian, H. M. (1973) 'The epidemiology of anorexia nervosa', *Psychol. Medicine*, 3, 200–3.

Kerfoot, M. (1979) 'Parent–child role reversal and adolescent suicidal behaviour', *Journal of Adolescence*, 2, 337–43.

Kerfoot, M. (1984) 'Suicidal behaviour: adolescents and their families'; in Wedge, P. (ed.) *Social Work – Research Into Practice*, BASW, Birmingham.

Kerfoot, M. (1986) 'Family therapy and psychotherapy following suicidal behaviour by young adolescents', in Diekstra, R. & Hawton, K. (eds) *Suicide in Adolescene*, Martinus Nijhoff, Dordrecht.

Kifer, R. Lewis, M., Green, D. & Phillips, E. (1974) 'Training predelinquent youths and their parents to negotiate conflict situations', *J. App. Behav. Analysis*, 7, 357–364.

Kolvin, I., MacKeith, R. & Meadow, S. R. (1973) *Bladder Control and Enuresis*, Heinemann, London.

Kraemer, S. (1987) 'Working with parents: casework or psychotherapy', *J. Child Psychol. Psychiat.*, 28, 2, 207–13.

Lask, J. & Lask, B. (1981) *Child Psychiatry and Social Work*. Tavistock, London.

Lawrence, M. (1984) *The Anorexic Experience*, The Women's Press, London.

McAuley, R. (1982) 'Training parents to modify conduct problems in their children', *J. Child Psychol. Psychiat.*, 23, 3, 335–42.

McAuley, R. & McAuley, P. (1977) *Child Behaviour Problems*, Macmillan, London.

McAuley, R. & McAuley, P. (1980) 'The effectiveness of behaviour modification with families', *Br. J. Social Work*, 10, 1, 43–54.

Mawby, R. I. (1977) 'Truancy: data from a self-report survey', *Durham and Newcastle Research Review*, 8, XXXIX, 21–34.

Morgan, P. (1979) *Delinquent Fantasies*, Maurice Temple Smith, London.

O'Connor, D., (1983) *Glue Sniffing and Volatile Substance Abuse: Case Studies of Children and Young Adults*, Gower, Aldershot.

Patterson, G. R. (1982) *Coercive Family Process*, Castalia, Oregon.

Pratt, J. (1983) 'Folklore and fact in truancy research: some critical comments on recent developments', *Brit. J. Criminology*, 23, 336–53.

Prins, H. (1985) 'Literature review: an abuse of some substance? *Br. J. Social Work*, 15, 403–8.

Pritchard, C. & Butler, A. (1975) 'Influence of the youth tutor upon teachers' perception of some maladjusted behaviour, *Child: Care, Health and Development* 1, 251–61.

Pritchard, C. & Butler, A. (1978) 'Teachers' perceptions of school phobic and truant behaviour and the influence of the youth tutor', *Journal of Adolescence*, 1, 273–82.

Pritchard, C., Fielding, M., Choudry, N., Cox, M. & Diamond, I. (1986) 'Incidence of drug and solvent abuse in 'normal' fourth and fifth year comprehensive school children – some socio-behavioural characteristics', *Br. J. Social Work*, 16, 341–51.

Richman, N. (1981) 'A community survey of characteristics of 1–2 year olds with sleep disruptions', *J. Am. Acad. Child Psychiat.*, 20, 281–91.

Richman, N., Stevenson, J., Graham, P. (1975) 'Prevalence of behaviour problems in 3 year old children: an epidemiological study in a London borough', *Journal of Child. Psychol. Psychiat.*, 16, 277–87.

Robins, L. N. (1986) *Deviant Children Grown Up*, Williams & Wilkins, Baltimore.

Rose, G. & Marshall, A. F. (1975) *Counselling and School Social Work*, Wiley, Chichester,

Rutter, M. (1975) *Helping Troubled Children*, Penguin, Harmonsworth.

Rutter, M. (1980) *Changing Youth In A Changing Society*, Harvard University Press, Cambridge, Mass.

Rutter, M. Tizard, J. & Whitmore, K. (1970) *Education, Health, and Behaviour*, Longman, London.

Rutter, M. Cox, A., Tupling, C., Berger, M., & Yule, W., (1975) 'Attainment and adjustment in two geographical areas: I – the prevalence of psychiatric disorders', *Br. J. Psychiatry*, 126, 493–509.

Sluckin, A., (1975) 'Encopresis: a behavioural approach described', *Social Work Today* 5, 643–6.

Strang, J. (1983) 'Problem drug-taking', *Medicine International*, 1, 1621–4.

Stuart, I. R. & Wells, C. F. (eds) (1981) *Self-Destructive Behaviour in Children and Adolescents*, Van Nostrand Reinhold, New York.

Thompson, A. (1982) 'Managing solvent abuse', *Community Care.*, 14 Oct. 1982.

Walker, H. & Beaumont, B. (eds) (1985) *Working with Offenders*, Macmillan, London.

Watson, J. (1986) *Solvent Abuse: The Adolescent Epidemic?* Croom Helm, London.

West, D. J. & Farrington. D. P. (1973) *Who Becomes Delinquent?*, Heinmann, London.

Wolff, S. (1977) 'Non-delinquent disturbances of conduct', in Rutter, M. & Hersov, L. (eds) *Child Psychiatry: Modern Approaches*, Blackwell. Oxford.

Wolff, S., (1981) *Children Under Stress*, Penguin, Harmondsworth.

Yates, R. (1985) 'Addiction: an everyday disease', in Lishman, J. (ed.) *Approches to Addiction*, Kogan Page, London.

Young, J. (1971) *The Drug Takers*, Paladin, London.

Index